Leader's Guide

Church • Prayer • Seeking God • The World • Stewardship • Witness • Call

7 Things Christians Do

Creeds and Deeds Part II

FAITH in Motion

Abingdon Press

Joy Butcher-Winfree

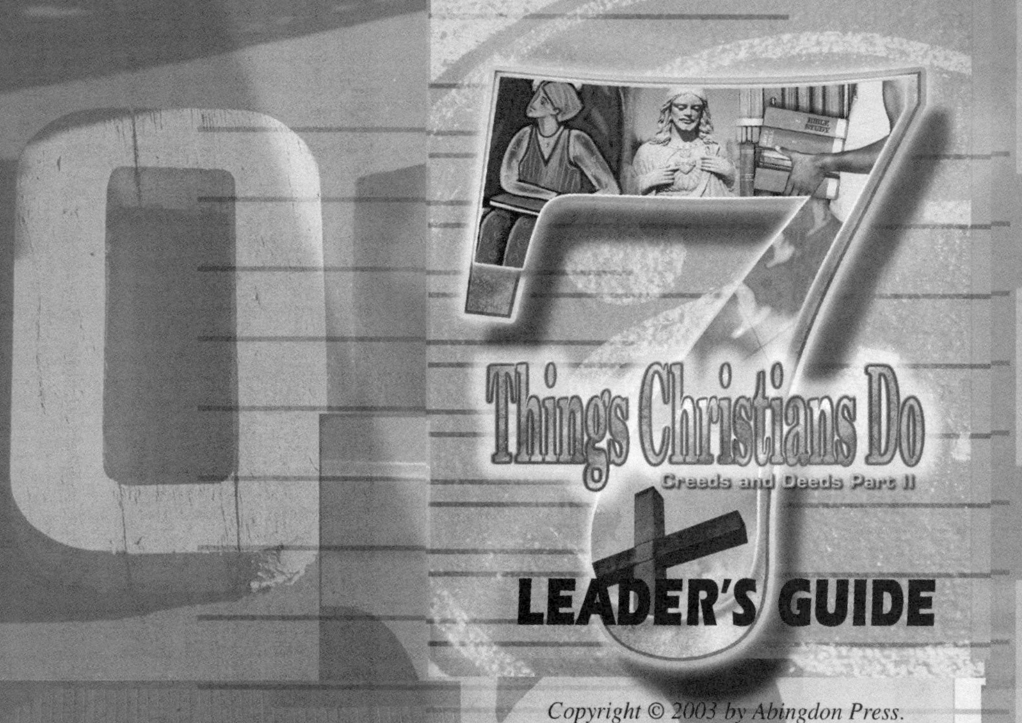

This book is printed on acid-free, recycled paper.

04 05 06 07 08 09 10 11 12—10 9 8 7 6 5 4 3 2

MANUFACTURED IN THE UNITED STATES OF AMERICA

Development Team
Jola Bortner
Rusty Cartee
Harriette Cross
Tim Gossett
Sharon Meads
Beth Miller
David Stewart

Editorial Team
Crystal A. Zinkiewicz, Senior Editor
Tim Gossett, Development Editor
Josh Tinley, Associate Editor

Design Team
Keely J. Moore, Design Manager
Kelly Chinn, Designer

Administrative Staff
Neil M. Alexander, Publisher
Harriet Jane Olson, Vice President/Editor of Church School Resources
Bob Shell, Director of Youth Resources

CONTENTS

How to Use Faith in Motion

Leader's Guide

Information and Formation

Topic and Key Verse
This Life-to-Bible curriculum starts with important topics for junior highs and goes to God's Word.

Take-Home Learning
The goal for the session is clear.

Younger Youth and This Topic
Find out more about your youth and how they are likely to connect with this concern.

Theology and This Topic
How does Christian faith and tradition help us to understand and deal with the concern?

You and the Scripture
Our being formed as a Christian through Bible reflection and prayer is essential for our teaching.

Transformation

The ultimate goal: Youth will become more fully devoted disciples of Jesus Christ.

Do I Have to Go to Church?

Topic: Belonging to a Church Community

Scriptures: Acts 4:32-34; Hebrews 10:24-25

Key Verse: "And let us consider how to provoke one another to love and good deeds, not neglecting to meet together, as is the habit of some, but encouraging one another, and all the more as you see the Day approaching" (Hebrews 10:24-25).

Take-Home Learning: The church, like a family, provides a nurturing environment that helps us grow.

Younger Youth and the Topic

Do I have to go to church? Almost every parent, pastor, or youth leader has heard this question from a youth at one time or another. As adolescents become more independent, they begin questioning ideas they have inherited from their parents or guardians. It is healthy and normal for youth to voice such questions and concerns.

This time of questioning is fundamental in the development of critical thinking skills that enable youth to take ownership of their faith. On one hand, questioning the need for church attendance could suggest that a youth is resistent, disinterested in conforming to a particular model of society. On the other hand, it could simply express an adolescent's need to have some choice in what he or she does and how he or she lives out the Christian faith. Youth are not inclined to participate in something that has no personal significance or meaning and are less likely to enjoy an activity that they did not choose for themselves.

Our challenge, then, is to help our youth discover what is important about being a part of a family of faith. We want youth to look forward to worship and church functions, not to think of these activities as obligations. Younger youth often rebel against such "have-to-do" things. Instead of telling youth they must go to church, we need to help youth discover what participation in the church community means to them.

Theology and the Topic

People choose their church today based on many factors—the music, the nursery, the preaching, and so on. But now that so many of these benefits of church can be found elsewhere, why should we bother to go at all? The answer for us now is no different than the answer given by the early

Leader's Guide

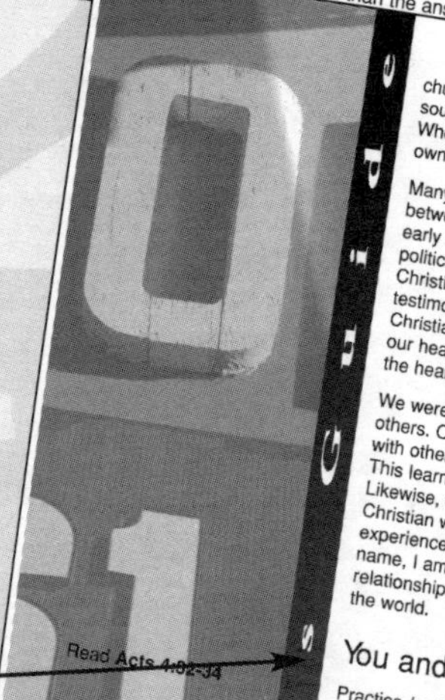

church. In Acts Luke tells us the early believers were of one heart and soul and that they held everything in common (Acts 2:43-47; 4:32-37). When people share the same heart and soul and relinquish private ownership of their possessions, they discover community.

Many groups throughout the world place boundaries (real or imagined) between themselves and others and call themselves a community. The early church was set apart by boundaries, some of which were imposed politically from the outside and others that came from within. These early Christians were best distinguished by their common proclamation and testimony of the resurrection of Jesus Christ. The same is true for Christians today. Through the promise of the Holy Spirit, God dwells in our hearts. An awareness of God's presence in our lives will reveal to us the heart and soul we share with God and all of creation.

We were created to be in relationship, first with God and then with others. Our faith grows more fully when it is shared and experienced with others. We learn a great deal from those whose lives touch ours. This learning helps develop our faith and our identity as Christians. Likewise, our lives touch the lives of others, helping them along on their Christian walk. Jesus stressed the importance of these shared experiences when he said, "Where two or three are gathered in my name, I am there among them" (Matthew 18:20). Through our relationships, God molds us and tranforms us so that we can transform the world.

You and the Scripture

Practice *lectio divina* (divine reading) with the Scriptures for each session in this volume:

- First, read the key passage slowly and prayerfully. Let the words within the Word jump out at you as you read. Consider the depth with which you read by profoundly dwelling on one individual word or phrase that catches your attention. Reflect on your life and the choices you've made as you read.
- Second, meditate. Let the special word or phrase that you discovered in the first reading of the passage sink into your soul. Put your mind, will, and emotions into meditating on that single word or phrase. View it from all angles, and let whatever comes to your mind about this word or phrase take root in your consciousness.
- Third, pray the text. Respond to the reading in the form of a prayer. In essence "pray back to God," engaging God in dialogue.
- Fourth, contemplate. Rest. Allow the text to work itself into you. Let it soak into your deepest being. Don't seek further insight, just cherish your encounter with God.

Leader's Guide

8

7 Things Christians Do: Creeds and Deeds, Part II

Overview Chart
Look here for the big picture of the session. Also note the key activities, just in case time is tight.

Jump Right In!
The opening activity engages youth as they arrive.

Experience It!
Learning activities give youth a common base for making new connections.

Explore Connections
What do the Scriptures have to say? What does this mean for my life? What is a Christian to do?

Take the Challenge
The learnings are not just for Sunday!

Encounter the Holy
Ritual and mystery, prayer and commitment change hearts.

Student Journal and Reproducible Handouts

Life Focus
Topics deal with issues and concerns important to junior high youth.

Spirit Forming
The journal provides practical help and scriptural encouragement.

Group Friendly
Printed Scripture references, discussion questions, and handouts facilitate participation by individuals and small groups.

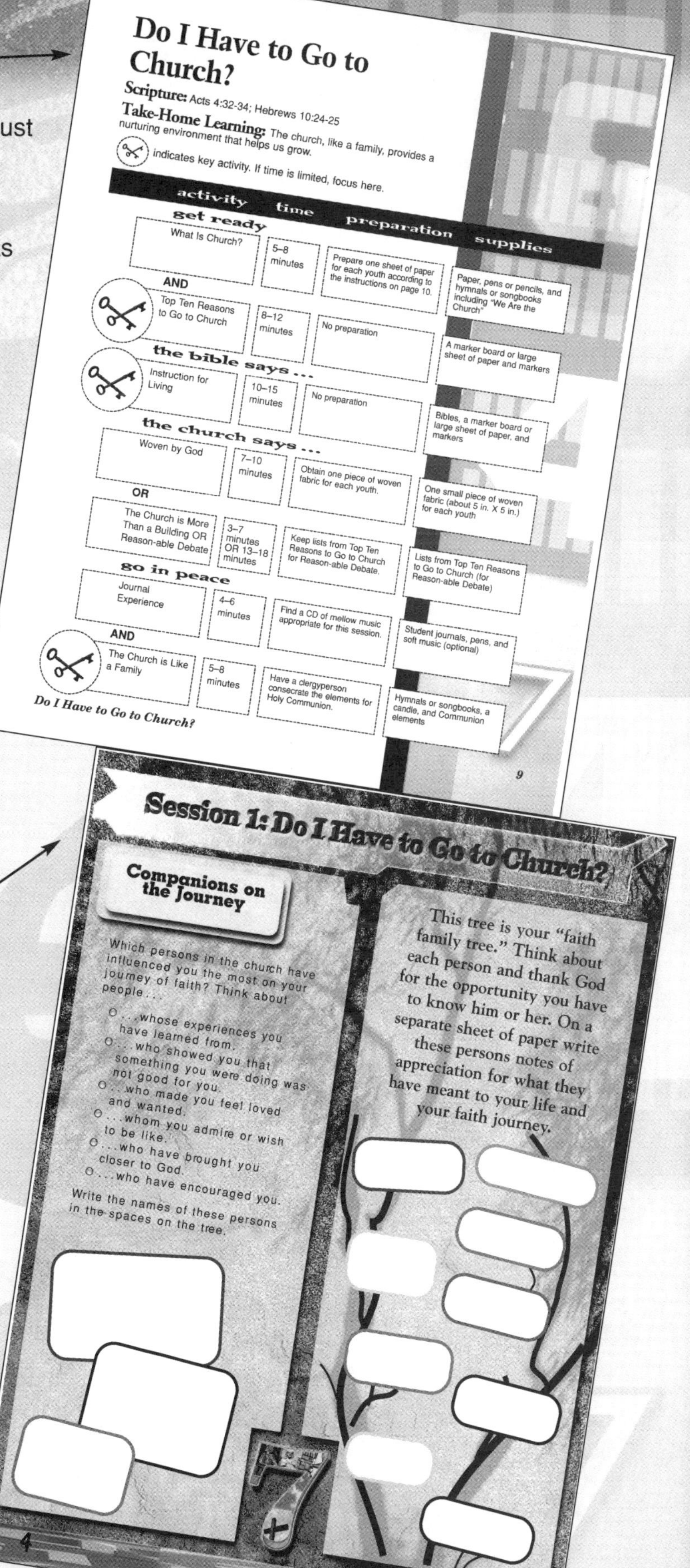

Do I Have to Go to Church?

Scripture: Acts 4:32-34; Hebrews 10:24-25

Take-Home Learning: The church, like a family, provides a nurturing environment that helps us grow.

(key symbol) indicates key activity. If time is limited, focus here.

activity	time	preparation	supplies
get ready			
What Is Church?	5–8 minutes	Prepare one sheet of paper for each youth according to the instructions on page 10.	Paper, pens or pencils, and hymnals or songbooks including "We Are the Church"
AND			
(key) Top Ten Reasons to Go to Church	8–12 minutes	No preparation	A marker board or large sheet of paper and markers
the bible says . . .			
(key) Instruction for Living	10–15 minutes	No preparation	Bibles, a marker board or large sheet of paper, and markers
the church says . . .			
Woven by God	7–10 minutes	Obtain one piece of woven fabric for each youth.	One small piece of woven fabric (about 5 in. X 5 in.) for each youth
OR			
The Church is More Than a Building OR Reason-able Debate	3–7 minutes OR 13–18 minutes	Keep lists from Top Ten Reasons to Go to Church for Reason-able Debate.	Lists from Top Ten Reasons to Go to Church (for Reason-able Debate)
go in peace			
Journal Experience	4–6 minutes	Find a CD of mellow music appropriate for this session.	Student journals, pens, and soft music (optional)
AND			
(key) The Church is Like a Family	5–8 minutes	Have a clergyperson consecrate the elements for Holy Communion.	Hymnals or songbooks, a candle, and Communion elements

Do I Have to Go to Church?

9

Session 1: Do I Have to Go to Church?

Companions on the Journey

Which persons in the church have influenced you the most on your journey of faith? Think about people . . .

- . . . whose experiences you have learned from.
- . . . who showed you that something you were doing was not good for you.
- . . . who made you feel loved and wanted.
- . . . whom you admire or wish to be like.
- . . . who have brought you closer to God.
- . . . who have encouraged you.

Write the names of these persons in the spaces on the tree.

This tree is your "faith family tree." Think about each person and thank God for the opportunity you have to know him or her. On a separate sheet of paper write these persons notes of appreciation for what they have meant to your life and your faith journey.

4

5

What's a Christian to Do?

Christians are children of God, disciples (or students) of Jesus, believers of the Word, and missionaries of compassion. We expect awareness, readiness, obedience, fortitude, humbleness, compassion, and commitment from one another. Yet at the same time, we struggle to find our own answers to the question, "What's a Christian to do?" It's no wonder that helping youth find life-changing answers to this important question is a humongous endeavor.

Wouldn't it be much easier if we had a checklist that described in detail exactly how to be faithful disciples, that gave us step-by-step instructions on how to live as a Christian? Surprise! In the words of an old fast food commercial: "It's in there!" These answers are in the Bible, but we do have to search for them. As we struggle with difficult questions, the answers become our own and we discover unique ways to live them out.

As a teacher, you are blessed with the opportunity to tease out these answers with your youth, to help them struggle with how Christians live out their call faithfully. Be prepared for their understanding to differ from yours or to be entirely nontraditional. Youth have unique and quite wonderful ways of applying Scripture to their lives. Your job is not to be a "lightning rod" of knowledge but a "divining rod" of transformation. Trust the Holy Spirit as you teach these sessions and be open to insights that God provides you and your youth as you struggle together to live the Christian faith.

Youth have unique and quite wonderful ways of applying Scripture to their lives. Your job is not to be a "lightning rod" of knowledge but a "divining rod" of transformation.

The questions that form the outline for these sessions are ones that most Christians ask at some point along their spiritual journeys. These seven questions are by no means the only ones asked by Christians growing in their faith, but they can serve as a jumping off point for your youth by encouraging them to honestly struggle with how they are to live as Christians.

Before teaching these sessions, read the following foundational texts: Genesis 1:27-28; Micah 6:8; Luke 12:31. These Scriptures provide a framework in which you and your youth can discover how each of you is being called to live faithfully as a child of God.

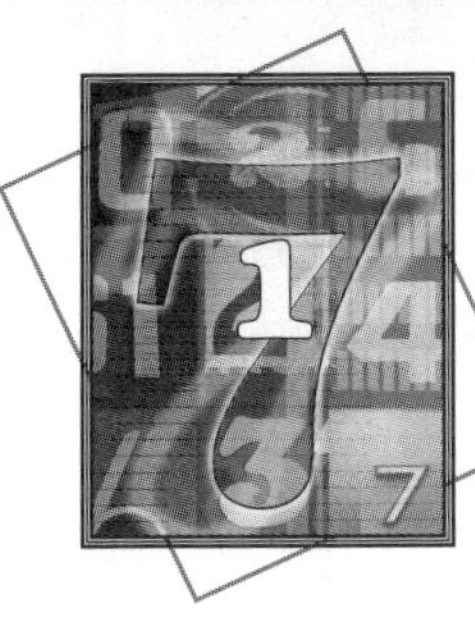

Do I Have to Go to Church?

Topic: Belonging to a Church Community

Scriptures: Acts 4:32-34; Hebrews 10:24-25

Key Verse: "And let us consider how to provoke one another to love and good deeds, not neglecting to meet together, as is the habit of some, but encouraging one another, and all the more as you see the Day approaching" (Hebrews 10:24-25).

Take-Home Learning: The church, like a family, provides a nurturing environment that helps us grow.

Younger Youth and the Topic

Do I have to go to church? Almost every parent, pastor, or youth leader has heard this question from a youth at one time or another. As adolescents become more independent, they begin questioning ideas they have inherited from their parents or guardians. It is healthy and normal for youth to voice such questions and concerns.

This time of questioning is fundamental in the development of critical thinking skills that enable youth to take ownership of their faith. On one hand, questioning the need for church attendance could suggest that a youth is resistant, uninterested in conforming to a particular model of society. On the other hand, it could simply express an adolescent's need to have some choice in what he or she does and how he or she lives out the Christian faith. Youth are not inclined to participate in something that has no personal significance or meaning and are less likely to enjoy an activity that they did not choose for themselves.

Our challenge, then, is to help our youth discover what is important about being a part of a family of faith. We want youth to look forward to worship and church functions, not to think of these activities as obligations. Younger youth often rebel against such "have-to-do" things. Instead of telling youth they must go to church, we need to help youth discover what participation in the church community means to them.

Theology and the Topic

People choose their church today based on many factors—the music, the nursery, the preaching, and so on. But now that so many of these benefits of church can be found elsewhere, why should we bother to go at all? The answer for us now is no different than the answer given by the early

church. In Acts Luke tells us the early believers were of one heart and soul and that they held everything in common (Acts 2:43-47; 4:32-37). When people share the same heart and soul and relinquish private ownership of their possessions, they discover community.

Many groups throughout the world place boundaries (real or imagined) between themselves and others and call themselves a community. The early church was set apart by boundaries, some of which were imposed politically from the outside and others that came from within. These early Christians were best distinguished by their common proclamation and testimony of the resurrection of Jesus Christ. The same is true for Christians today. Through the promise of the Holy Spirit, God dwells in our hearts. An awareness of God's presence in our lives will reveal to us the heart and soul we share with God and all of creation.

We were created to be in relationship, first with God and then with others. Our faith grows more fully when it is shared and experienced with others. We learn a great deal from those whose lives touch ours. This learning helps develop our faith and our identity as Christians. Likewise, our lives touch the lives of others, helping them along on their Christian walk. Jesus stressed the importance of these shared experiences when he said, "Where two or three are gathered in my name, I am there among them" (Matthew 18:20). Through our relationships, God molds us and transforms us so that we can transform the world.

You and the Scripture

Read **Acts 4:32-34**

Practice *lectio divina* (divine reading) with the Scriptures for each session in this volume:

- First, read the key passage slowly and prayerfully. Let the words within the Word jump out at you as you read. Consider the depth with which you read by profoundly dwelling on one individual word or phrase that catches your attention. Reflect on your life and the choices you've made as you read.
- Second, meditate. Let the special word or phrase that you discovered in the first reading of the passage sink into your soul. Put your mind, will, and emotions into meditating on that single word or phrase. View it from all angles, and let whatever comes to your mind about this word or phrase take root in your consciousness.
- Third, pray the text. Respond to the reading in the form of a prayer. In essence "pray back to God," engaging God in dialogue.
- Fourth, contemplate. Rest. Allow the text to work itself into you. Let it soak into your deepest being. Don't seek further insight, just cherish your encounter with God.

Do I Have to Go to Church?

Scripture: Acts 4:32-34; Hebrews 10:24-25

Take-Home Learning: The church, like a family, provides a nurturing environment that helps us grow.

 indicates key activity. If time is limited, focus here.

activity	time	preparation	supplies
get ready			
What Is Church?	5–8 minutes	Prepare one sheet of paper for each youth according to the instructions on page 10.	Paper, pens or pencils, and hymnals or songbooks including "We Are the Church"
AND			
Top Ten Reasons to Go to Church (key activity)	8–12 minutes	No preparation	A markerboard or large sheet of paper and markers
the bible says ...			
Instruction for Living (key activity)	10–15 minutes	No preparation	Bibles, a markerboard or large sheet of paper, and markers
the church says ...			
Woven by God	7–10 minutes	Obtain one piece of woven fabric for each youth.	One small piece of woven fabric (about 5 in. X 5 in.) for each youth
OR			
The Church Is More Than a Building OR Reason-able Debate	3–7 minutes OR 13–18 minutes	Keep definitions from What Is Church? or lists from Top Ten Reasons to Go to Church.	Definitions from What Is Church? or lists from Top Ten Reasons to Go to Church
go in peace			
Journal Experience	4–6 minutes	Find a CD of mellow music appropriate for this session.	Student journals, pens, and soft music (optional)
AND			
The Church Is Like a Family (key activity)	5–8 minutes	Have a clergyperson consecrate the elements for Holy Communion.	Hymnals or songbooks, a candle, and Communion elements

Leader's Guide

get ready

Provide sheets of paper prepared accordingly, pens or pencils, and hymnals or songbooks including the song "We Are the Church."

What Is Church? (5–8 minutes)

As the youth gather, give each person a sheet of paper with the words "The Church is . . ." printed at the top. Ask the youth to think of different ways to complete the sentence defining the word *church*. Emphasize that there are no right or wrong answers, but encourage the youth to list descriptions they have picked up from others as well as their own definitions of church.

Ask for a few volunteers to read their definitions, then sing a few verses of "We Are the Church."

AND

Provide a markerboard or large sheet of paper and markers.

With a large number of youth, divide into smaller groups and have each group create its own top ten list.

Top Ten Reasons to Go to Church (8–12 minutes)

Ask the youth to brainstorm the top reasons for going to church. Allow humorous and serious responses and encourage youth to be creative. Write their ideas on a markerboard or large sheet of paper. As a group, narrow the list down to the top ten reasons and rank these reasons from one (most important) to ten (least important).

Next, have the youth brainstorm reasons for not going to church. Ask them to think about what they have heard others say about not attending church, problems some people might have with the church, or reasons people think church is not important. Again, have youth choose and rank the top ten reasons. Be careful not to judge their answers, and don't differentiate between personal ("I think . . .") and nonpersonal ("I heard someone say . . .") answers.

the bible says ...

Provide Bibles, a markerboard or large sheet of paper, and markers.

It is OK if you don't use every single Scripture or if one Scripture is assigned to more than one pair.

Instruction for Living (10–15 minutes)

Divide youth into pairs and assign each pair one of the Scriptures below. Ask the pairs to read their Scripture and to discuss how it relates to their reasons for going to church.

- **Proverbs 27:17** ("Iron sharpens iron, and one person sharpens the wits of another.")
- **Matthew 18:20** ("For where two or three are gathered in my name, I am there among them.")
- **Acts 4:32-34** ("Now the whole group of those who believed were of one heart and soul. . . .")
- **Romans 12:4-6** ("For as in one body we have many members . . .")
- **Romans 12:18** ("If it is possible . . . live peaceably with all.")
- **1 Corinthians 12:24b-26** ("If one member suffers, all suffer together . . . ; if one member is honored, all rejoice together. . . .")
- **Ephesians 4:15-16** ("Speaking the truth in love, we must grow up in every way into him who is the head, into Christ. . . .")
- **Hebrews 10:24-25** ("And let us consider how to provoke one another to love and good deeds. . . .")

STUDENT JOURNAL

Joy Butcher-Winfree

Abingdon Press

CONTENTS

Companions on the Journey

Which persons in the church have influenced you the most on your journey of faith? Think about people . . .

- **. . . whose experiences you have learned from.**
- **. . . who showed you that something you were doing was not good for you.**
- **. . . who made you feel loved and wanted.**
- **. . . whom you admire or wish to be like.**
- **. . . who have brought you closer to God.**
- **. . . who have encouraged you.**

Write the names of these persons in the spaces on the tree on page 5.

to Go to Church?

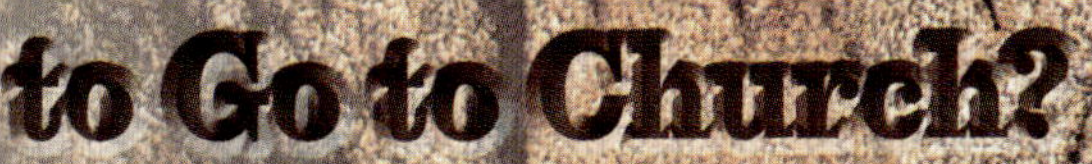

This tree is your "faith family tree." Think about each person and thank God for the opportunity you have had to know him or her. On separate shcets of paper write these persons notes of appreciation for what they have meant to your life and your faith journey.

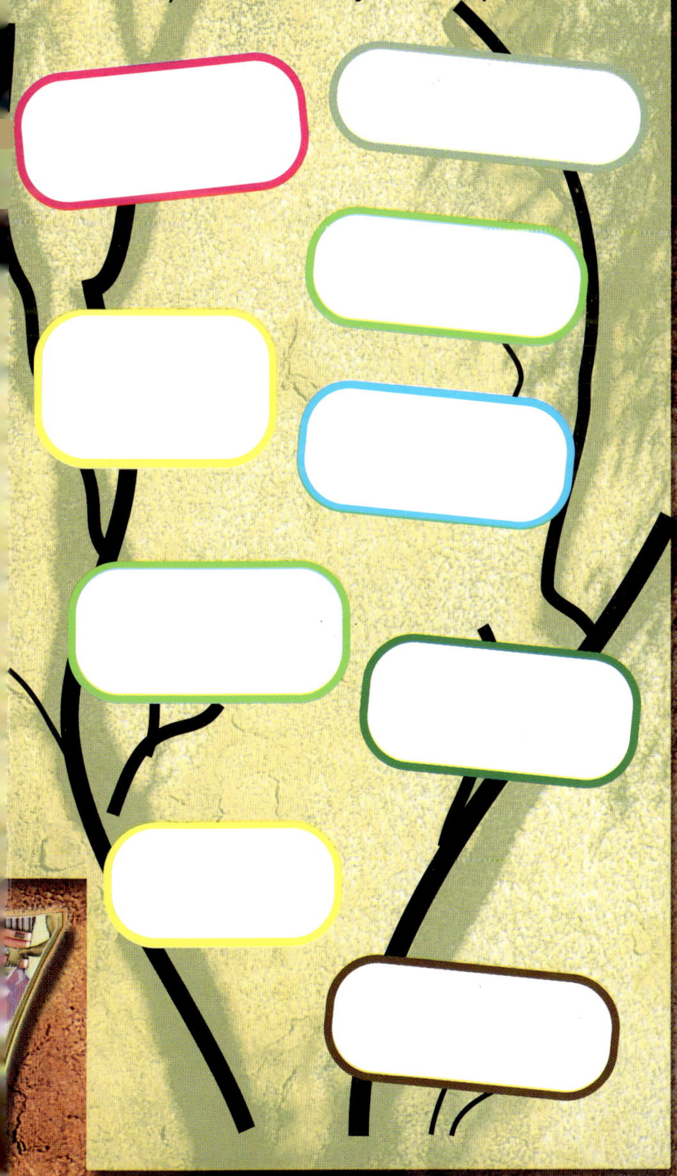

Deep Thoughts

"Let one who cannot be alone beware of community . . . Let one who is not in community beware of being alone."—
Dietrich Bonhoeffer

- **What do you think Dietrich Bonhoeffer is trying to say?**

"I have community with others and I shall continue to have it only through Jesus Christ. The more genuine and the deeper our community becomes, the more surely will everything between us recede, the more clearly and purely will Jesus Christ and his work become the one and only thing that is vital between us."—
Dietrich Bonhoeffer

- **Who are people with whom you share a vital relationship in Jesus Christ?**

Both quotes taken from *Life Together* by Dietrich Bonhoeffer (Harper and Row, New York, 1954). Bonhoeffer (1906–1945) was a German clergyman, professor, and theologian who was executed for opposing the Nazi regime.

Are You an Island or an Isthmus?

"No man is an island, entire of itself; every man is a piece of the continent, a part of the main."—

John Donne, Meditation XVII

Island people . . .

- . . . try to do everything by themselves.
- . . . sometimes think they can get by without God.
- . . . isolate themselves physically and emotionally.
- . . . forget that what they do has an impact on others.

Isthmus people . . .

- . . . are unique individuals with unique identities but are still deeply connected to others.
- . . . value friendships and relationships.
- . . . remember their connection to God.
- . . . aren't afraid to let others know when they need help.
- . . . consider the impact of their words and actions on others or on the earth.

What kind of person was Jesus?

What kind of person are you?

My Prayer Life

Complete each of the following sentences about your prayer life.

1. God answered my prayer when I prayed about ____________________________

___________________________________ .

2. God answered that prayer by

____

___________________________ .

3. I didn't feel like God answered my prayer when ___________________

_____________________________ .

4. I like to pray [where] ____________

_____________________________ .

5. I like to pray [when] __________

__________________________ .

6. I like to pray [how] ______________________
____
____.

7. The biggest need I should pray about right now is ______________________
____
____.

"Prayer—secret, fervent, believing prayer—lies at the root of all personal godliness."

William Cary

What do you think this quote means?

Try rewriting this quote in your own words. (Hint: "Fervent" means "intense.")

Finger Labyrinth

The labyrinth is an ancient tool for prayer and meditation. Usually, it is outlined on a floor or carpet, and individuals walk its course while praying silently.

Trace your fingers slowly around this labyrinth. Try to clear your mind and listen for God. Think about your spiritual journey or repeat a phrase over and over such as, "God, fill my mind with your peace, and my heart with your love."

What Are You Doing Here?

During the meditation, what thoughts, ideas, or messages came to mind? Describe your experience:

"What we need is a desire to know the whole will of God, with a fixed resolution to do it."
John Wesley

What do you think this means?

God's E-mail Address?

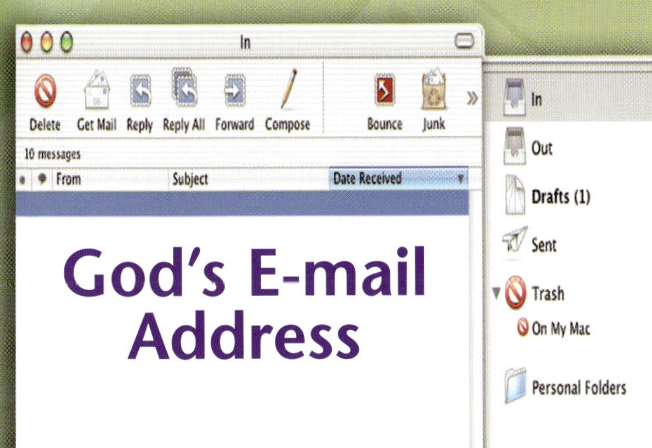

God's E-mail Address

- Deuteronomy 4:9
- 1 Chronicles 16:29
- Psalm 119:105
- Luke 11:1-13
- 1 Kings 19:1-13
- Psalm 19:1-4
- Matthew 18:20
- John 13:1-14

Match each of the following e-mail addresses with one of the Scriptures above:

- prayer@listen.God ________________
- service@listen.God ________________
- worship@listen.God ________________
- scripture@listen.God ________________
- silence@listen.God ________________
- community@listen.God ________________
- everydaylife@listen.God ________________
- creation@listen.God ________________

How are your experiences with God similar to the experiences recorded in these Scriptures?

Is God only to be found in the church? Why or why not?

Wait for the Lord

"Wait for the Lord; be strong, and let your heart take courage; wait for the Lord!"
Psalm 27:14

God's sense of timing is much different than ours. Sometimes we grow anxious waiting for the Lord to answer our prayers.

- When have you become impatient waiting on a word from God?

- Think of one problem or situation you would like to take to God. (You may be waiting impatiently for God's solution to this problem at this very moment.) Write down all your concerns about this situation, and in silence lay them before God:

Three Questions to Ask Yourself

Here are three good questions to ask yourself when you have a tough decision to make. Think about the situation you wrote about on page 14 as you answer these questions.

1. What messages or advice have friends, family members, and others in my life offered me?

2. What gifts or strengths has God given me that help me make informed and faithful decisions?

3. What do I want for myself, and how does that make me feel?

Am I Personally Responsible?

Humans tend to be good at "buck-passing"—blaming someone else for the problems of the world or believing someone else is responsible for taking care of a certain problem.

When have you "passed the buck" instead of accepting your personal responsibility?

Christians believe that God holds us accountable for our actions. We could think of sin as a failure to own up to our faults or a failure to do the right thing. It's difficult to accept some responsibility for the wrongs of the world, but it's a more honest way to live, and one that can make a real difference!

Caring 4 Creation

- How are you responsible for taking care of creation?

- How responsibly do you live as a resident of God's creation? Rate yourself on a scale from *1* to *10* in each of the following categories:

  1) the foods you eat (and how much)

  2) the clothes you wear

  3) how much you use or waste compared to how much you reuse or recycle

  4) how you give of yourself for others and to make your community a better place

- List 4 changes you can make to become a better caretaker of creation. Commit to making these changes.

Caring 4 Others

In the movie ***Patch Adams***, Patch, a doctor with nontraditional but inspiring ideas about healing, describes his philosophy of caring for his patients: "You treat a disease, you, you lose. You treat people and I guarantee you win!"

- Why do we sometimes distance ourselves from those God calls us to serve?

- When you remind yourself that all people and all things come from God, how does your thinking change? How does your way of life change?

- List 4 changes you can make that will help you better care for others. Commit to making these changes.

Caring 4 Myself

"Do you not know that you are God's temple and that God's Spirit dwells in you? . . . God's temple is holy and you are that temple."
(1 Corinthians 3:16, 17b)

How well do you care for yourself? Below, rate yourself on a scale from *1* to *10* in each of the four categories. Put an X on each of the lines to indicate how you're doing:

PHYSICALLY

0 ________________________________ 10

EMOTIONALLY

0 ________________________________ 10

MENTALLY

0 ________________________________ 10

SPIRITUALLY

0 ________________________________ 10

- List 4 changes you can make that will help you better care for yourself. Commit to making these changes.

Are You a Hoarder or Helper?

Read Acts 5:1-11

Ananias (AN-uh-NIGH-uhs) and ***Sapphira*** (suh-FIGH-ruh) kept a little for themselves, but they told everyone else that they had given all that they had. When their secret was revealed, they died. Perhaps the knowledge that they had not fully valued their community of faith was more than they could bear.

- **What might you be holding back from God or hoarding for yourself?**

- **Which is easiest for you to use to help others and to glorify God, your money, time, or talents? Why?**

- **What secrets are you keeping for fear that others will think less of you?**

Take time to tell God about those things that are keeping you from fully committing to your faith. Pray for God's help as you work toward making better use of your money, time, and talents.

"Some people know the cost of everything and the value of nothing."*

What does this statement mean to you?

Below list some of the talents or abilities you have worked hard to develop:

*based on a quote from Oscar Wilde

Pay It Forward

In the movie, ***Pay It Forward****, Mr. Simonet challenges his students to come up with an idea that can change the world. A student, Trevor, accepts the challenge. Creating a concept called "pay it forward," he decides that if he could just help three people who would in turn help three people, who would help three more people, he could start a movement that would change everyone.

This ancient principle of discipleship, investing oneself in the lives a small number of people who in turn invest themselves in the lives in others, is laughed at by the seventh graders in Trevor's class. They believe that such attempts are "utopian" or "naive" and don't account for human nature.

Even Trevor doubts his plan when he does not see immediate results. True to life, seeds planted take time to blossom. But when they do, beauty springs forth.

Answer the questions on page 23, listing ways that you could "pay it forward" by using your money, time, and talents to help others.

* *Pay It Forward* (Warner Brothers, 2000). Directed by Mimi Leder, screenplay by Leslie Dixon.

- **How can I use my time for God?**

- **How can I use my money for God?**

- **How can I use my talents for God?**

My Stories of Faith

Reflect on your faith story as you answer the following questions:

- **Think of one person who was important to your spiritual formation. What did this person teach you?**

- **Think of a time when God or Christ became incredibly real for you. Describe that situation:**

- **What doubts have you had, and what questions have you asked about your faith? How have you handled these doubts and questions?**

to Share My Faith

- Think of your favorite Bible stories. How have these stories shaped your faith? How do they connect to your life?

- Mary of Bethany anointed Jesus with a fragrant and expensive ointment (John 12:1-8). What unexpected and extravagant act of love can you perform for Jesus?

- What can you do this week to reflect Jesus' love for you?

You Are My Witnesses

In Isaiah 43:10, God says, "You are my witnesses." Witnessing is, simply, reporting one's encounters God. Witnessing should be more personal that just quoting Bible verses or giving a sermon. (Actually, it doesn't even have to be that hard.) When you witness, you should simply tell others about your experiences.

- **How have you experienced God's grace in your life or in the lives of others? How has God changed your life or the life of someone you know well?**

- **Think of one story you could tell about how God's love has helped you along your faith journey. Who would benefit from hearing your story? When could you tell your story to this person?**

- **How are you a witness to the presence of God in your life?**

"I have told the glad news of deliverance
in the great congregation;
see, I have not restrained my lips;
as you know, O Lord.
I have not hidden your saving help
within my heart;
I have spoken of your faithfulness
and your salvation;
I have not concealed your steadfast
love and your faithfulness
from the great congregation."

Psalm 40:9-10

- **How do you think people see your faith lived out in your words and actions?**

- **Whom do you know who needs to hear about God's love through Christ? How could you tell these persons your story?**

The Call

The Lord desires intensely
that we love him
And seek his company.
So much that from time to
time
He calls us to draw near to
him.

The call comes through
words spoken by other
good people,
Or through sermons,
Or through what is read in
books,
Or through the many things
that are
heard and by which God
calls,
or by illnesses and trials,
or in enjoying the beauty of
creation,
or also through a truth that
he teaches
during the brief time we
spend in prayer.

Teresa of Avila (1515–1582)
from *Interior Castle**

*Translation from *Meditations with Teresa of Avila* by Camille Cambell (Bear & Co, 1985).

Look Back on God's Call

- **Briefly look back over the other sessions in this journal. How have these sessions helped you better hear God's call to live the Christian life?**

- **God often speaks to us through other persons. Whom has God used to speak to you?**

- **When has God spoken to you through a book you were reading? When has God spoken to you through music, movies, or other art-forms?**

- **What hardships, trials, or problems have brought you closer to God? How has God spoken to you through bad situations?**

This book is printed on acid-free, recycled paper.

05 06 07 08 09 10 11 12—10 9 8 7 6 5 4 3 2

MANUFACTURED IN
THE UNITED STATES OF AMERICA

Student Journal

Church • Prayer • Seeking God • The World • Stewardship • Witness • Call

7 Things Christians Do

Creeds and Deeds Part II

FAITH in Motion

Joy Butcher-Winfree

- **When has a sermon, Sunday school lesson, or church activity helped you better understand God's call?**

- **When have you seen and heard God in the beauty and magnificence of God's creation?**

- **When has God spoken to you directly in your prayers?**

NOTES

NOTES

Student Journal

ISBN 0-687-08326-5

9 780687 083268 90000

Abingdon Press

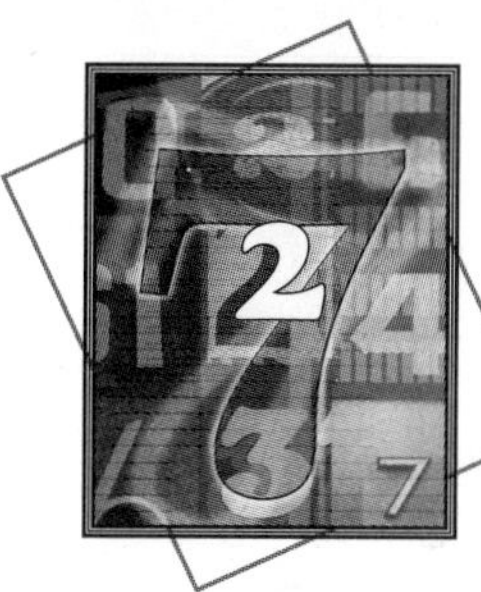

How Do I Pray Without Ceasing?

Topic: Prayer

Scriptures: Luke 11:5-10; 18:1; Acts 2:42; Romans 12:9-13; 1 Thessalonians 5:16-18

Key Verse: "Rejoice always, pray without ceasing, give thanks in all circumstances, for this is the will of God in Christ Jesus for you" (1 Thessalonians 5:16-18).

Take-Home Learning: Praying without ceasing means being involved in a consistently intentional loving relationship with God.

Younger Youth and the Topic

Prayer is a difficult concept for many youth. Some youth cannot understand having a conversation with someone they cannot see with their eyes or hear with their ears. God probably won't respond with an instant message or a voice mail. Other youth may have no experience praying on their own, as adults have always prayed on their behalf. Some youth have daily prayer routines (at meals, before bedtime, or in the morning) but have not been introduced to the idea of praying anywhere at any time. For any of these youth the concept of praying without ceasing may seem impossible.

You can help your youth understand that praying without ceasing means living a life of prayer. You can help them understand prayer as an opening of their lives to God and not just as a set of words. To do so, introduce youth to different forms of prayer and encourage them to pray in different settings. This will help them to associate every part of their life with prayer and to experience a life of prayer without ceasing. Youth may need a variety of images, postures, and words to make prayer real in their lives.

Theology and the Topic

Richard Foster wrote:

> To pray is to change. This is a great grace. How good of God to provide a path whereby our lives can be taken over by love and joy and peace and patience and kindness and goodness and faithfulness and gentleness and self-control. The movement inward comes first because without interior transformation the movement up into God's glory would overwhelm us and the movement out into ministry would destroy us.[1]

Practice *lectio divina* as you read **Luke 11:5-10.** (See page 8 for instructions.)

Jesus compares such a life of prayer to an old widow who refuses to accept her helplessness. She stands up to the injustices of her life, and through her persistence is offered justice (Luke 18:1-8). How often we give up after we have prayed once or twice! We need to keep asking, keep seeking, keep knocking. John Calvin wrote, "We must repeat the same supplications not twice or three times only, but as often as we have need, a hundred and a thousand times. . . . We must never be weary in waiting for God's help."[2]

Prayer may be defined as the act of seeking God through earnest request. The belief in and practice of prayer acknowledges God's authority as well as our human vulnerability. In the early church writings instructions and descriptions of prayer are teamed with concepts of neighborly love, fellowship, breaking of bread, and love of enemies. Included in the character of prayer are suggestions of admiration, rejoicing and forgiveness. Thus prayer is not simply the act of saying words or assuming a prescribed posture; it is a humble, intentional and consistent relationship entreating God's presence in our lives.

Although the character and discipline of prayer varies, all prayer involves attentive awareness and openness to God's grace. Love moves through the unexpected just as it moves through the everyday events of our lives. That God is not visible or audible to the petitioner does not mean God is not there. The call for never-ending prayer is a call for an ever-vigilant and constant awareness of the nearness of God.

You and the Scripture

Prepare for this lesson by doing the following exercise:

- Imagine you see the Risen Lord before you; then imagine you hear him address to you with this invitation: "Watch and pray."
- Do not reply immediately to his invitation. Instead, imagine him repeating those words again and again. Let those words resound in your whole being.
- Keep listening to those words. Let them challenge you, and let them bring you to a response, until your response is ready to burst from you. Then say to the Lord what your heart is aching to say.
- Spend a few moments in silence. Then think about these questions:
    1. How might my prayer life be similar to the prayer lives of my youth?
    2. What insights can I offer to help my youth understand prayer as a way of life?

How Do I Pray Without Ceasing?

Scripture: Luke 11:5-10; 18:1; Acts 2:42; Romans 12:9-13; 1 Thessalonians 5:16-18

Take-Home Learning: Praying without ceasing means being involved in a consistently intentional loving relationship with God.

 indicates key activity. If time is limited, focus here.

activity	time	preparation	supplies
get ready			
What Is Prayer? (key activity)	9–11 minutes	No preparation	Paper and pens or pencils
the bible says . . .			
Instruction for Living (key activity)	10–12 minutes	Review the Scriptures listed on page 16.	Bibles, paper, and pens or pencils
the church says . . .			
Listening to God	6–9 minutes	Review the instructions on page 17.	No supplies
AND			
Meeting God in Everyday Life (key activity)	14–18 minutes	Map out a short walking route in the neighborhood surrounding your church.	Index cards and markers
go in peace			
Journal Experience	4–8 minutes	No preparation	Student journals, pens, and a CD and CD player (optional)
OR			
Body Prayer	5 minutes	Review the instructions on page 18.	No supplies

get ready

Provide paper and pens or pencils.

What is Prayer? (9–11 minutes)

As youth arrive, divide them into groups of three or four. Give each group a sheet of paper and ask the groups to write down things that people . . .

- do incessantly or seem to do without stopping. (*Possible answers: whining, talking, eating*)
- actually do constantly or without stopping. (*Possible answers: breathing, pumping blood, growing older*)
- might like to do without stopping. (*Possible answers: vacationing, sleeping, feeling happy*)

After a few minutes, have each group present its list. Ask: "Is it possible to pray without stopping?" (If any youth answer, "yes," ask: "How?")

Say: "Today we're going to explore praying without ceasing. In living the Christian life, we are called to be constantly in prayer with God. What does it mean to be in prayer? Paul says: 'The Spirit helps us in our weakness, for we do not know how to pray as we ought, but that very Spirit interceded with sighs too deep for words' (Romans 8:26-27).

"So get comfortable, close your eyes, and try to experience what this scripture is talking about. In silence, let's seek God by praying for whatever comes to mind." After several minutes in silence, ask:

- Was it difficult thinking of something to pray about?
- What came to your mind?
- Was it uncomfortable being silent for that long? Why or why not?

the bible says . . .

Provide Bibles, paper, and pens or pencils.

Instruction for Living (10–12 minutes)

Hand out Bibles, paper, and pens or pencils. Divide the class into pairs, and assign each pair one of the following scriptures:

- **Luke 11:5-10**
- **Luke 18:1-8**
- **Acts 2:42**
- **Romans 12:9-13**
- **1 Thessalonians 5:16-18**

Ask the youth to read their Scripture with their partner and to work together to write their verse(s) in their own words. Give the youth a few minutes to work, then encourage each pair to share its paraphrase with the rest of the class.

Then ask:

- What do these Scriptures have to say about prayer?
- How is prayer a part of the Christian life?
- What does it mean to pray without ceasing?

Listening to God (6–9 minutes)

Ask: "When you were silent during the opening prayer, what ideas came to mind? Where do you think these ideas came from?"

Say: "Prayer is about listening to God, not just talking to God. Prayer means being intentional and giving God our attention so that we might hear what it is God is saying to us. Prayer is both active and passive: active in that we pursue God and passive in that God pursues us."

Have the youth pair off (or have them stay in the pairs from the previous activity). Say: "We're going to put ourselves in God's shoes." Ask the older person in each pair to play the role of the speaker and the younger person to be the non-listener. Instruct the speaker to tell the non-listener about the best day of his or her entire life; instruct the non-listener to do anything they can to keep from listening. Give the pairs a couple minutes to work before asking the participants to switch roles. Then ask:

- What was it like trying to tell your partner about the best day of your life?
- How does feel to talk to someone who doesn't want to listen?
- How can you know that God listens to your prayers?
- How can you know when you are listening to God?
- How was your conversation with your partner like conversations you've had with God? How was it different?

AND

Meeting God in Everyday Life (14–18 minutes)

Say: "When we learn to appreciate God's gifts and God's wondrous creation, we learn to be constantly in prayer to God. To give you a better idea of continual thanksgiving, I'm going to take you on a walk."

Take the group on a silent walk through the surrounding neighborhood. Instruct the youth to pay close attention to nature, houses and buildings, and the actions and facial expressions of passersby. Encourage youth to say a word of thanksgiving to God every time they notice something such as the blue sky, the green grass, an animal scurrying by, a person's smile, and so on. Remind them to be specific in their thanks. (Instead of simply saying, "Thank you, God, for the trees," one could say, "Thank you, God, for the trees because they give us shade in the summer.")

Spend between five and ten minutes on your walk. When you return, ask volunteers to tell about what they noticed that they were thankful for.

Hand out index cards and markers. Ask each youth to write the phrase, "Thank you, God, for this day," on his or her card and to decorate the cards as they would like. Encourage the youth to pray this prayer when they wake each morning. Tell them to put their cards on a bathroom mirror, a bedside table, or another place where the cards will be noticed.

Provide index cards and markers.

go in peace

Provide student journals and pens. A CD and CD player is optional.

When doing this activity, be sensitive to youth with handicapping conditions.

Leader's Guide

Journal Experience (4–8 Minutes)

Hand out student journals. Give the youth about five minutes to complete the activities on pages 8–11 in their journals. If you would like, play some quiet music in the background.

OR

Body Prayer (5 minutes)

Say: "To close, we will offer ourselves to God with a body prayer, expressing our feelings through movements and gestures."

Have the youth spread throughout the room. Read aloud the following instructions slowly, pausing to allow the youth to perform each action.

- Stand up with your hands hanging loosely at your sides, and your head bowed, eyes closed.
- Remember that you are in the presence of God.
- Raise your arms slowly and stretch them wide toward the heavens.
- Slowly lift your head until you are facing the heavens.
- Open your eyes slowly and gaze toward God. Hold this posture for a few moments.
- Let your hands drop gently back to their original position, and let your head fall. Pause for a moment and take a deep breath.
- Now, let's give devotion to God. Stand up with your hands hanging loosely at your sides, your head bowed, and your eyes closed.
- Again, remember that you are in the presence of God.
- Raise your hands very slowly until they are stretched out in front of you, parallel to the floor.
- Slowly turn your hands so that your palms face upward.
- Raise your head slowly until you are looking up toward the sky.
- Open your eyes slowly and gaze upward. Hold this posture.
- Let your hands drop gently back to their original position, and let your head fall. Pause for a moment and take a deep breath.
- Give honor to God by standing with your hands hanging loosely at your sides, your head bowed, and your eyes closed. Slowly bend toward the ground, letting your hands drop toward the earth.
- Bending your knees, fall gently to the ground and place your hands flat on the floor. Hold this posture.
- Rise and straighten your knees until you are standing, bent at the waist. Slowly raise your upper body until you are standing straight with your arms at your side. Look forward and open your eyes.
- Take a deep breath, and release it slowly.

Say: "When you pray this way, you give power and body to your prayer. This style of prayer is helpful when your mind is distracted and you are having trouble praying with words. Try it again this week on your own!"

[1] From *Prayer: Finding the Heart's True Home,* by Richard J. Foster (Harper San Francisco,1992); page 6.

[2] From *Sermons on the Epistle to the Ephesians,* by John Calvin (Banner of Truth Trust, 1975); page 683.

Do You Have God's E-mail Address?

Topic: Connecting with God in all things

Scripture: Deuteronomy 4:9; 1 Kings 19:11-13; 1 Chronicles 16:29; Psalm 19:1-4; 119:105; Matthew 18:20; Luke 11:1-13; John 13:1-14

Key Verse: "'Go out and stand on the mountain before the Lord, for the Lord is about to pass by.' . . . And after the fire a sound sheer silence. . . . Then there came a voice to him . . ." 1 Kings 19:11-13

Take-Home Learning: silence@listen.God; prayer@listen.God; service@listen.God; worship@listen.God; creation@listen.God; scripture@listen.God; community@listen.God; everydaylife@listen.God

Younger Youth and the Topic

The lives of many younger youth are filled with difficult choices and decisions. They often feel pressured to please so many different people—parents, youth leaders, teachers, coaches, friends, peers, and themselves. Think back to when you were their age. Do you remember how so many decisions seemed almost life-threatening? Youth need help discerning the consequences of their many decisions.

Younger youth also need help seeing how God is at work in their lives, offering guidance. Few youth can do this on their own. After all, even adults tend to have a limited understanding of God's presence. Youth might believe that God is far beyond their reach or is only present in the church building. Help your youth discover God in many different places: in people, Scripture, silence, nature, art and music, events, and prayer. Help them discover that God is closer to them than they might imagine, and that God is ready and waiting to help them.

Theology and the Topic

Today's world is full of technological wonders that can overwhelm the imagination. Computer chips, satellites, lasers, and microwaves are used in so many ways that we work and play with them on a daily basis. The Millennial Generation in the United States has never known a time without remote control or electric can openers. Twenty-first century technology is quickly turning us into a push-button society. We've reached a point where we can buy anything we desire with a credit card and a computer. But how do we get in touch with God?

At a time when e-mail and chat rooms are a part of many adolescents' daily routines, God's e-mail address is a natural metaphor. Imagine how human spirituality would change if God were literally to send and receive e-mail. How convenient! However, if we pay attention to Elijah's mountaintop experience, we discover that God's presence was most recognizable in the absence of earthly tools and gadgets. 1 Kings 19:12-13 describes God's being present "in the sound of sheer silence." If we understand prayer as a discipline of consistent, intentional, and mutual communication and understand Christian decision-making as the result of prayerful discernment, we might think of God's e-mail address as silence@listen.God.

However, silence often disrupts our way of life. Use of this address might require shutting down our computers, CD players, games, and other devices to bring our questions before God. When we find God by sitting in silent prayer; meditating on our questions and concerns without prejudice, expectation, or judgment; or allowing God to freely transform our lives into gifts of grace; we send a message to the prayer@listen.God inbox. When we help others (service@listen.God) we encounter God. In worship (worship@listen.God) we experience God and connect God's timeless messages to our particular time and situation. God can be found in creation (creation@listen.God), which John Calvin expressed when he wrote, "Wherever you cast your eyes, there is no spot in the universe wherein you cannot discern at least some sparks of God's glory."[1] We find God in Scripture (scripture@listen.God), in relationships with other believers (community@listen.God), and in ordinary everyday living (everydaylife@listen.God). The opportunity to connect with God is all around us . . . *if* we're ready to listen.

You and the Scripture

Practice *lectio divina* as you read **1 Kings 9:11-13.** (See page 8 for instructions.)

Prepare for this lesson with the following exercise:

- Imagine seeing the Risen Christ before you, and then imagine you hear him address you with the words of God's response to Elijah: "What are you doing here, (your name) . . ."
- Do not reply immediately to his question. Imagine you hear him repeat those words again and again. Let them spread throughout your entire being.
- Keep listening to those words. Allow them to challenge you, to bring you to a response, until your response is ready to burst from you. Then say to the Lord what your heart is aching to say.
- Spend a few moments in silence. Then ask yourself these questions:

    1) How might my youth answer to the question, "What are you doing here, (your name)?"

    2) How does God help me in my decision making?

Do You Have God's E-mail Address?

Scripture: Deuteronomy 4:9; 1 Kings 19:11-13; 1 Chronicles 16:29; Psalm 19:1-4; 119:105; Matthew 18:20; Luke 11:1-13; John 13:1-14

Take-Home Learning: silence@listen.God; prayer@listen.God; service@listen.God; worship@listen.God; creation@listen.God; scripture@listen.God; community@listen.God; everydaylife@listen.God

 indicates key activity. If time is limited, focus here.

activity	time	preparation	supplies
get ready			
Where Is God? (key activity)	5–10 minutes	Cover one wall of your meeting space with large sheets of paper.	Large sheets of paper and markers
AND			
What Are You Doing Here? (key activity)	8–12 minutes	Read and review 1 Kings 19.	Bibles, student journals, and pens
the bible says ...			
E-mail Addresses (key activity)	6–9 minutes	Review the Scriptures on page 23 and consider the optional activity on page 23.	Bibles, student journals, pens, a markerboard or large sheet of paper, a marker, and index cards
the church says ...			
I Need an Answer	8–15 minutes	Duplicate the Choices—A Case Study handout from page 49 (optional).	Index cards, pens, and handouts (optional)
go in peace			
Journal Experience	4–5 minutes	No preparation	Student journals, pens, and a CD and CD player (optional)
AND			
I Have Decided to Follow Jesus	3–5 minutes	No preparation	Hymnals or songbooks including the song, "I Have Decided to Follow Jesus"

get ready

Provide large sheets of paper, and markers.

Where Is God? (5–10 minutes)

Beforehand, cover one wall of your meeting space with large sheets of paper. Toward the top, write, "Where God Can Be Found."

As the youth arrive, invite them to respond to the question, "Where can God be found?" by writing graffiti-style words and phrases, or by drawing pictures of where they imagine God is at work or where they have experienced God in their lives.

AND

Provide Bibles, student journals, and pens.

What Are You Doing Here? (8–12 minutes)

Beforehand, review 1 Kings 19. Introduce the text to your youth by saying, "Elijah was a prophet who, by prophesying, made Queen Jezebel very angry—angry enough for her to want to kill him. Out of fear Elijah fled into the mountains and hid in a cave, seeking direction from God." Then ask a youth to read aloud 1 Kings 19:11-13.

Ask the youth to think of a reason why they need direction from God. As they reflect on the issues or situations that come to mind, have them close their eyes and get into a comfortable position. Then read each of the statements below, pausing between each one to allow students to reflect.

- Imagine you see the Risen Christ before you, and that he calls out your name, followed by, 'What are you doing here? What do you want from me? How can I help you? What is it you need from me?'
- Do not reply immediately. Instead, imagine that you hear him repeat those questions again and again. Let his words spread throughout your entire being.
- Keep listening to those words. Allow them to challenge you, to bring you to a response, until your response is ready to burst from you. Then say to the Lord what your heart is aching to say.

Allow youth to spend a few moments in silence. Then pass out student journals. Give the youth a few minutes to complete What Are You Doing Here? on page 12.

the bible says ...

Provide Bibles, student journals, and pens. A markerboard or large sheet of paper, a marker, and index cards are optional.

E-Mail Addresses (6–9 minutes)

Ask: "If God had an e-mail address, what do you think it would be?" Allow youth to respond. (You might record some of their answers on a markerboard or large sheet of paper.) Then ask, "How would our relationship with God be different if God did have an e-mail address?"

Say: "It would be great if we could connect with God through e-mail, but since humans haven't invented a server that can handle that kind of traffic, we must look elsewhere. Elijah found God in the silence on top of Mt. Horeb. So you might think of God's e-mail address as silence@listen.God. Let's look at other Scriptures that tell us where God can be found and how God can help us to make difficult decisions."

Divide your class into eight groups and assign each group one of the passages below. Each Scripture says something about where God can be found. Ask the groups to think about where God is found in their verses and have them create an e-mail address for God based on their findings. (Addresses used in the student journal activity are underlined in the list below.)

- **Deuteronomy 4:9:** everydaylife@listen.God (*God speaks to us in the everyday-ness of our lives.*)
- **1 Kings 19:1-13:** silence@listen.God (*Sometimes we cannot hear God until we've let go of all the distractions.*)
- **1 Chronicles 16:29:** worship@listen.God (*Worship is at the heart of a life with God.*)
- **Psalm 19:1-4:** creation@listen.God (*God becomes known in God's handiwork.*)
- **Psalm 119:105:** scripture@listen.God (*As the 18th century Bishop Tikhon of Zodonsk said, "Whenever you read the Gospel, Christ himself is speaking to you."*)
- **Matthew 18:20:** community@listen.God (*Other people convey God's grace and presence.*)
- **Luke 11:1-13:** prayer@listen.God (*Prayer is always a conversation with God.*)
- **John 13:1-14:** service@listen.God (*We discover that when we help others, we find God.*)

Ask each group to report the e-mail address it came up with and where God can be found according to its Scripture. Hand out student journals and have youth complete God's E-mail Address on page 13.

Option (8–12 minutes): Liven up this activity by writing the eight sample e-mail addresses on index cards and hiding them around the church. Try to hide the cards in places related to their subject matter. For example, prayer@listen.God could be hidden at the altar, scripture@listen.God by a stack of Bibles, and so on.

Hand out student journals and Bibles. Tell the groups to look up each passage listed on page 13 of their journals and to search for locations in the church related to that passage. When they find a card, have them write down that e-mail address in their journals next to the corresponding Scripture.

If you have a small number of youth, assign one Scripture to each youth; or divide into fewer groups and assign more than one Scripture to each group.

Provide Bibles, index cards prepared accordingly, students journals, and pens.

I Need an Answer (8–15 minutes)

Say: "When we struggle with making good decisions, we need to look to God. We can find God in our surroundings and in the persons we interact with. We also can find God's answers in our own gifts and strengths. Sometimes it is helpful to ask ourselves, 'What do I want?' or, 'How will this decision make me feel?' Persons who have been faced with similar decisions can help us see the consequences of certain

the church says ...

Provide index cards and pens. Copies of the Choices—A Case Study handout from page 49 are optional.

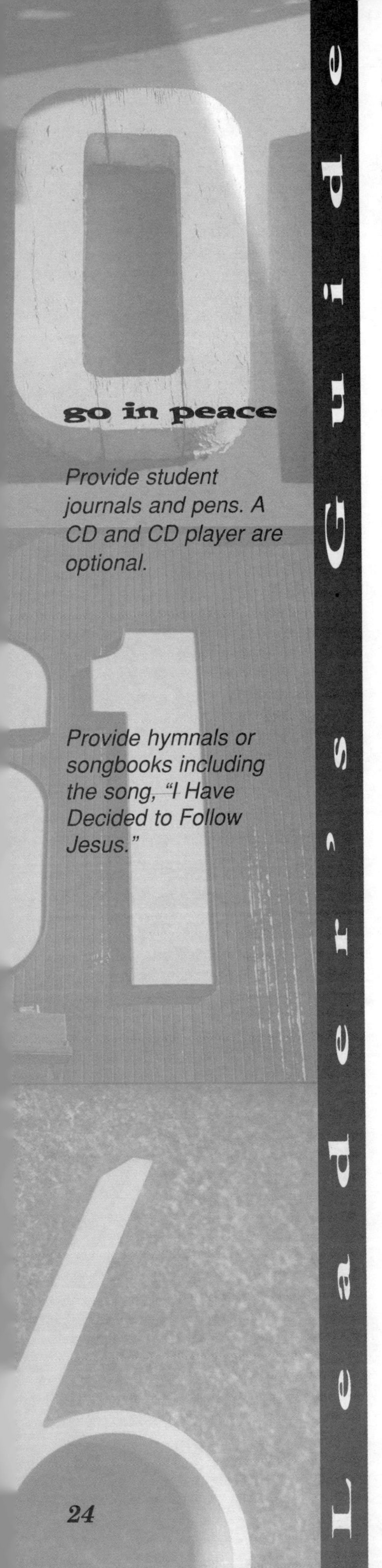

actions. Sometimes it is even helpful to act out or imagine the consequences of different decisions."

Hand out index cards and ask the youth to write down a difficult decision that they're facing. Let them know that their cards will be read aloud. (If time is limited, use the situation described on the Choices—A Case Study handout from page 49.) Collect the cards, shuffle them, and choose one to read aloud. Adapt the questions from page 49 to guide a discussion about the possible consequences of each difficult decision. Go through as many decision-making scenarios as possible.

Provide student journals and pens. A CD and CD player are optional.

Journaling Experience (4–5 minutes)

Allow youth a few minutes to complete the activities on pages 13–14 of their student journals. You might play some soft music in the background to help them focus.

AND

Provide hymnals or songbooks including the song, "I Have Decided to Follow Jesus."

I Have Decided to Follow Jesus (3–5 minutes)

Gather the youth in a circle. Sing the chorus to the song "I Have Decided to Follow Jesus."

Then, in turns, invite individuals to complete this sentence: "I have decided to follow Jesus this week by . . ."

Invite the others to respond to each statement with: "No turning back, no turning back."

End this prayer time with a brief prayer asking for God's guidance throughout the week as your youth are faced with difficult decisions. Pray that youth will be opened to the many ways in which God communicates with them.

[1] From *Institutes of the Christian Religion*, by John Calvin (Westminster John Knox Press,1960).

What Is My Personal Responsibility?

Topic: Caring for creation

Scripture: Genesis 1:1–2:4a; 9:1-7; Psalm 8; Matthew 25:31-46; 1 Corinthians 3:9-17

Key Verse: "Then God said, 'Let us make humankind in our image, according to our likeness; and let them have dominion over the fish of the sea, and over the birds of the air, and over the cattle, and over all the wild animals of the earth, and over every creeping thing that creeps upon the earth'" (Genesis 1:26).

Take-Home Learning: God intends for us to understand and care for God's creation. We are created in the image of God and are called to see others as God's good creation.

Younger Youth and the Topic

Younger youth are growing in individuality and independence and must learn to live responsibly and to account for their actions. Since we live in a world where so much is disposable, each of us must recognize how we harm God's creation and how we can help God's creation. While society tempts us to believe that the earth's resources have been placed here by God for our enjoyment, as Christians we believe that we are stewards of God's creation.

Some youth may have a difficulty understanding God's call to care for the earth and for others. Many young adolescents have always been cared *for*; they have always been dependent. Now they have reached an age when they seek to be *in*dependent, free from the boundaries established by their parents. While independence has its merits, responsible stewards recognize that all life is *inter*dependent. Youth who understand stewardship of creation at such a young age, will find it easier as adults to reject ways of living that exploit persons, cultures, and the environment.

Theology and the Topic

In the first creation story in Genesis, God creates all that is: the earth and sky, the oceans and land, the plants and animals, and human beings. Once this is accomplished, God commands humankind to "fill the earth to subdue it" and gives humans "dominion over" all creation. Unfortunately, some Christians have associated these words with governance or even exploitation, assuming permission to dominate the earth's resources and

Trivia Question: What's the first commandment in the Bible? (Hint: it's not one of the Ten Commandments. See Genesis 1.)

Practice *lectio divina* as you read **Genesis 1:1–2:4a**. (See page 8 for instructions.)

people. Others interpret God's instruction to "be fruitful and multiply" as a command to live as luxuriously and comfortably as possible.

However, God intends for us to live a life of "in-gathering" and expects us to care for all that God has created. "Be fruitful and multiply" refers not only to human reproduction but also to increasing the value and worth of all creation. Our interdependence with creation is implicit in the opening chapters of Genesis. The Hebrew word *adam* means "earth being" and is closely related to *adamah*, meaning land or earth. We need the earth and its fruits to survive, and the earth need us to replenish and nurture it to remain fruitful.

Just as we are connected to the earth, we are connected to one another by God. References to these connections and God's desire for us to live in relationship can be found throughout the Bible. For example, the Book of Psalms includes many hymns that remind us of the harmony among all of God's creatures. In Luke, Jesus reminds us to be faithful and diligent in managing what belongs to God (16:10-12). In Romans, Paul hopes that creation will be "set free from its bondage to decay and will obtain the freedom of the glory of the children of God" (8:21). These Scriptures remind us that the Christian community is called by God through Jesus Christ to a lifestyle that takes seriously the care of all of God's creation.

You and the Scripture

Read aloud Genesis 1:1—2:4a. Spend a moment silently reflecting on the creation of all things, about the earth and all that is in it, about other people, and about yourself in relationship to creation.

Consider these words of Anthony de Mello:

> It is only inasmuch as I am attuned to my own feelings that I am able to be aware of the feelings of others. It is only inasmuch as I am aware of my reactions to others that I am able to go out to them in love, without doing them any harm. When I become sensitively aware of my self I also develop a refined awareness of others.... Some of the great mystics tell us that when become aware of others, of that that surrounds us, we become mysteriously filled with the a sense of deep reverence. Reverence for God, reverence for life in all its forms, reverence for inanimate creation.... We no longer treat persons as things, things as things.[1]

Francis of Assisi was one such mystic. He recognized in the sun, the moon, the stars, the trees, the birds, and the animals as his brothers and sisters. They were members of his family and he would talk to them lovingly. If you have time this week, read more about his life or watch the movie *Brother Sun, Sister Moon.*

Become aware of everything around you and look for God in everything and everyone. Continuously thank God for all of creation. Think seriously about making some changes to your own lifestyle (such as recycling more, buying less, choosing organic foods, and so on) that will keep you mindful of God's command to be a good steward of God's creation.

What Is My Personal Responsibility?

Scripture: Genesis 1:1–2:4a; 9:1-7; Psalm 8; Matthew 25:31-46; 1 Corinthians 3:9-17

Take-Home Learning: God intends for us to understand and care for God's creation. We are created in the image of God and are called to see others as God's good creation.

 indicates key activity. If time is limited, focus here.

activity	time	preparation	supplies
get ready			
Whose Job Is It? (key activity)	5–8 minutes	Duplicate the Whose Job Is It? handout from page 50.	Handouts and pens or pencils
the bible says . . .			
Covenant (key activity)	10–15 minutes	Read and review Genesis 1:26-31; 9:1-7.	Bibles, paper, and pens or pencils
OR			
Environmental Art	9–12 minutes	No preparation	Bibles, paper, pens or pencils, and assorted art supplies
the church says . . .			
Care Chain	12–15 minutes	Cut several strips of scrap paper (of equal length).	Strips of paper, thin markers, a markerboard or large sheet of paper, student journals, and pens
AND			
Self-Care (key activity)	5–9 minutes	No preparation	Bibles, student journals, and pens
go in peace			
The Web of Life	6–8 minutes	Prepare index cards according to the instructions on page 30.	A ball of yarn and index cards prepared accordingly
AND			
Circle of Life	4–6 minutes	No preparation	Bibles and a candle

get ready

Provide copies of the Whose Job Is It? handout from page 50 and pens or pencils.

Whose Job Is It? (5–8 minutes)

As youth arrive, distribute the Whose Job Is It? handout from page 50. Ask the youth to complete it individually.

When everyone has finished, say: “Our lesson today concerns the question ‘What are my personal responsibilities as a Christian?’ On this handout, you were asked to decide whose responsibility you think these jobs are. Let’s look briefly at your responses.”

Discuss each question on the handout. Make the point that we all have a responsibility to care for one another and for all creation.

the bible says ...

Provide Bibles, paper, and pens or pencils.

Covenant (10–15 minutes)

Divide the youth into two groups, and pass out Bibles. Assign one group Genesis 1:26-31 and the other Genesis 9:1-7.

Say: “These passages are about covenant. A covenant is like a contract in that two or more parties make an agreement. As a group, read your Scripture and determine who is making the covenant, what is being agreed to, and what responsibilities the parties have.” Have the groups record these answers on a sheet of paper.

- **Genesis 1:26-31:** The covenant is between God and humankind. God gives humans dominion over creation but commands them to “be fruitful and multiply.”
- **Genesis 9:1-7:** The covenant is between God and Noah’s family (humankind). God gives Noah dominion over all living things but demands that people not eat the blood of an animal or shed the blood of a human.

Ask: “What do these covenants say about our personal responsibility for creation?”

Divide the youth into groups of two or three. Give each group paper and pens or pencils. Say: “In your groups, create a contract with God concerning the care of all of creation—the earth, all living things, yourself, and others. Think about what promises you could make that would show you are a faithful caretaker of God’s creation. Be as specific as you can but don’t make a contract you cannot live up to.”

As they work, encourage youth to be specific about the responsibilities they will undertake to improve the environment, themselves, and others. When they have finished, have the groups present their contracts.

OR

Provide Bibles paper, pens or pencils, and assorted arts supplies.

Environmental Art (9–12 minutes)

Have the youth look up Psalm 8. Ask a volunteer to read it aloud. Then say: “This Psalm is an example of a hymn praising God for all of creation." Invite the youth to create their own works of art that say something about protecting the environment God has given us. They can write a poem, rap, or song, draw a picture, create a dance, and so forth. Allow youth to work in groups of two or three if they would like.

If they are at a loss, suggest they write a "Five Senses Poem" using this easy format:

- Line 1: Write the name of the poem.
- Line 2: Write about the sights of creation.
- Line 3: Write about the sounds of creation.
- Line 4: Write about the smells of creation.
- Line 5: Write about the tastes and flavors of creation.
- Line 6: Write about the textures and feelings of creation.
- Line 7: Write the name of the poem again.

Give youth several minutes to work, then invite them to present their creations.

Care Chain (12–15 minutes)

the church says ...

Provide several strips of scrap paper (of equal length), thin markers, a markerboard or large sheet of paper, student journals, and pens.

Instruct the youth to do a dramatic reading of Matthew 25:31-46. Assign a narrator and one person to play the role of the "Son of Man." Divide the rest of the youth into two groups: One group will be the "blessed"; the other will be the "cursed."

Then say: "Not only is the care of the earth our responsibility, but so is caring for one another." Ask: "What does the Scripture have to say about caring for others?" Record answers on a markerboard or sheet of paper.

Invite the youth to create a "Care Chain." Ask each person to write on separate slips of paper different ways he or she helps others. These deeds may include everything from doing chores at home to taking part in community service projects. See how far your chain can reach.

Then hand out student journals and ask youth to complete the activities on pages 16–18. Allow youth to discuss their answers with partners or in small groups.

AND

Self-Care (5–9 minutes)

Provide Bibles, student journals, and pens.

Have the youth read 1 Corinthians 3:9-17 silently while you hand out student journals.

Say: "We should remember that we are each a part of God's creation, and that God desires that we care for ourselves. Using the 'Caring 4 Myself' activity on page 19 of your journal evaluate how well you care for yourself."

Invite the youth to name some of the changes they would like to make in their lives. Encourage youth to listen to one another's ideas and to add to their lists any good ideas that they hear. Feel free to add suggestions that are not mentioned. (For example, Sabbath rest, daily prayer, Bible study, worship, good works, time alone, and so on.)

Then encourage each youth to choose three items on his or her list to focus on in this coming week.

go in peace

Provide a ball of yarn and index cards featuring pictures of "examples of creation."

The Web of Life (6–8 minutes)

Before class, prepare a set of cards with various examples of creation including plants, animals, humans, and other elements such as the sun, the oceans, and so on. Make at least one card for each youth. (With a small group, make at least two cards for each youth.) Attach lengths of yarn to the cards so they can hang around the students' necks.

Gather the youth in a circle and hand out the cards. Hand one end of a ball of yarn to the youth wearing the "humans" card. Say: "Raise your hand if you are wearing a card that shows something humans need to survive." It is possible that multiple youth will raise their hands. Hand the ball of yarn to one of these youth. Then look at the card worn by the person with the yarn and repeat the process. For example, if the person was wearing a "vegetation" card you could ask for cards that show something vegetation needs to survive; or you could ask for cards of other creatures that need vegetation to survive.

Continue this process until all the cards have been used. The yarn should form a web. Say: "What would happen if one of these items were removed from the environment?" Ask one youth to drop the yarn and leave the circle. Then instruct anyone who was connected to that person to do the same. End with a discussion of the importance of each living thing in every habitat and environment.

AND

Circle of Life (4–6 minutes)

Provide Bibles and a candle.

Ask the youth to gather in a circle. Place a lit candle in the middle. Explain that the candle represents God's light to us in Jesus Christ. Ask the youth to name a part of creation for which they are thankful. Then encourage them to name a way they can increase the value or goodness of creation this week. For example, they might visit a shut-in, plant a tree, clean up trash in a park, and so on.

Then read aloud and in unison Psalm 67 as a closing prayer.

[1]From *Sadhana: A Way To God* by Anthony de Mello (Doubleday, 1978); page 53.

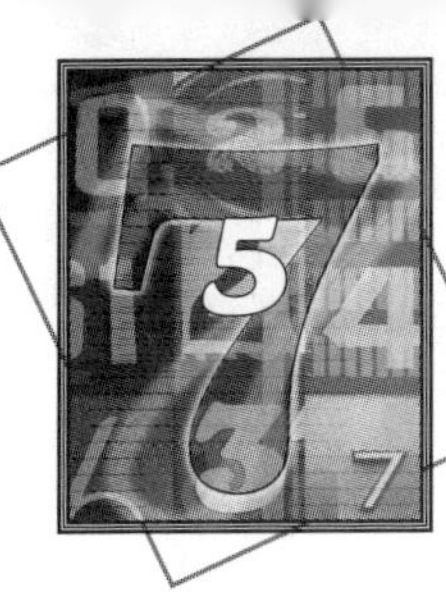

Can God Really Use My Money, Time, and Talents?

Topic: Giving of All We Have

Scripture: Matthew 6:19-21; Mark 12:41-44; Acts 4:32-35; 1 Corinthians 16:1-2; Ephesians 5:2

Key Verse: "Now the whole group of those who believed were of one heart and soul, and no one claimed private ownership of any possessions, but everything they owned was held in common" (Acts 4:32).

Take-Home Learning: By putting our money, time, and talents where our faith is, we proclaim what we believe about God.

Younger Youth and the Topic

Younger youth are well-aware of the power of money. For youth money often means success, power, or popularity. Having money enables youth to buy all of the top CDs and to see all the hit movies as soon as they are released. Money can divide youth, sometimes causing those with money to put themselves above those without. Youth without money and youth from poor families often feel powerless, frustrated, hampered, and isolated. Money involves choice and control, and youth understand this implicitly. Younger adolescents have a well-developed brand-consciousness and are well acquainted with the price on the tag. Yet they frequently have little real experience with money management and little understanding of the value of money. Youth also struggle with temptations to spend their money right here, right now. Saving for the future and sharing with others are not usually financial priorities for youth.

As a group, adolescents have become an earning and spending power to be reckoned with. Since they generally have few financial commitments, their spending is almost entirely discretionary. Too often, the habits that they form at this point in their lives carry over into adulthood. Thus it is critical for the church to talk openly with adolescents about the resources—financial and otherwise—that we all must manage. Youth need to learn how to be stewards of their time, money, and talents, all of which are gifts of God. They need to consider how they spend their resources in light of living a Christian life.

Theology and the Topic

The mind of any society is tied to its economy. Archeologists study architecture, trade routes, literature, lifestyles, and other behaviors of ancient people, thereby making accurate assumptions about their

Practice *lectio divina* as you read **Mark 12:41-44**. (See page 8 for instructions.)

economic behavior. In other words, all of these factors help archeologists understand the priorities of ancient peoples. We can do this for our society. By following the money, we see what is perceived as important and what is perceived as irrelevant.

Money, possessions, and time are all measures of corporate and individual power and priorities. Love, on the other hand, is the measure of our Christian faith. By allowing God's love to shape our use of our money, time, talents, and possessions we acknowledge our belief in God's love as the true power in our lives.

We see God's love reflected in the early church's priorities and beliefs. They were heavily influenced by Jesus' resurrection and were anxiously awaiting his return. As a result, they were willing to give their all to building the Christian community. While their behavior might seem cult-like if it were carried out in our own day, the account in Acts reveals a community without need—even though no one personally owned anything. The early Christians did not share and give because ownership and money were viewed as evil; they did so because they had heard the call of Jesus to live in community and to care for one another. This is what the stewardship of our resources is truly about.

You and the Scripture

This session will help youth understand that everything we have is a gift from God. Giving back to God shows one's gratitude for God's gifts.

As you prepare for this lesson, spend time thinking about the way you honor God with your money, time, and talents.

- How does your spending of money reflect your faith?
- How does your use of time reflect your faith?
- How does your expression of your talents reflect your faith?
- How might you change your use of money, time, and talent to better reflect your faith in God?

Can God Really Use My Money, Time, and Talents?

Scripture: Matthew 6:19-21; Mark 12:41-44; Acts 4:32-35; 1 Corinthians 16:1-2; Ephesians 5:2

Take-Home Learning: By putting our money, time, and talents where our faith is, we proclaim what we believe about God.

 indicates key activity. If time is limited, focus here.

activity	time	preparation	supplies
get ready			
The Good Life (key activity)	8–12 minutes	No preparation	Old magazines and newspapers, glue sticks, posterboard, and scissors
the church says . . .			
It Doesn't Belong to Me (key activity)	14–20 minutes	Think of examples of how people treat others' possessions differently than their own.	Paper, pens or pencils, and a bag of individually wrapped candies
the bible says . . .			
Where Is Your Heart? (key activity)	8–12 minutes	Duplicate the How I Use My Resources handout from page 51.	Bibles, handouts, and pens or pencils
OR			
In Jesus' Eyes	3–5 minutes	No preparation (unless you decide to purchase actual "widow's mites"—see page 35)	Bibles
go in peace			
Joyful Giving	8–13 minutes	Review the parable on page 36.	Student journals and pens
AND			
A Fragrance to God	4–6 minutes	No preparation	A candle and scented candles or potpourri

get ready

Provide old magazines and newspapers, glue sticks, posterboard, and scissors.

With a large number of youth, divide the youth into two or more groups and give each group its own posterboard to work on.

the church says ...

Provide paper, pens or pencils, and a bag of individually wrapped candies.

If youth have trouble getting started,here are a couple more examples:

- Most people are more careful about not making a mess in someone else's car than in their family's car.
- If you are the treasurer of a club at school, you would probably be more careful with the club's money than with your own.

The Good Life (8–12 minutes)

Beforehand, spread out (on tables or on the floor) a wide variety of old magazines and newspapers, glue sticks, and a large posterboard. As the youth arrive, ask them to look through the magazines and newspapers for images and words that represent how most people think of "the good life." Have them cut out these words and pictures and glue them to the posterboard.

After a few minutes, have everyone help clean up the mess. Then ask:

- Why did you choose certain words or images?
- Which of these words and images have to do with money? with possessions? with time? with abilities and talents?
- If you could have more money, more possessions, or more time, which would you choose? Why?
- What are some problems with how people often think of "the good life"? What words or pictures would represent your understanding of "the good life"?

It Doesn't Belong to Me (14–20 minutes)

Divide the youth into pairs and give each pair a sheet of paper and a pen or pencil. Say: "Sometimes, we treat other people's possessions differently than our own. For example, if I borrow a book from you, I'm likely to make sure nothing happens to it. But if it's my own book, I might dog-ear the pages to mark my place or let it get smashed on the bottom of my locker. I'd like you to work with your partner to think of other examples of how we treat others' possessions differently than our own. Try to think of some examples that don't involve borrowing possessions."

Give the youth three minutes to come up with examples, then ask each pair to report its answers. (Try to come up with some examples of your own to fill in any gaps, especially concerning use of time and talent.) As the pairs present, record the number of *original* examples each pair has created. (Eliminate any examples presented by more than one pair.)

Award a bag of candy to the winners, but say: "Since the prize is mine to begin with, you may only accept this prize if you use it in the way I ask you to. First, distribute the candy among the rest of the group; then walk around the church and give the candy away to others. Give away as much as you can in about three minutes, and then return. If someone asks why you're giving them candy, tell them you received it as a gift and you wanted to share."

When the winning pair returns ask them: "How did you feel when I told you that you had to give the candy away?"

Then ask the entire group: "What is it like giving away something that doesn't belong to you?"

Say: "Usually we think of our time, talents, and money as personal property that we can use as we like. But as Christians we need a different perspective. We believe that everything is God's and that we are just caretakers and managers, or stewards. Recognizing that all we have comes from God changes how we use our time, our talents, and our money. We discover that we're happier when we give those things away instead of when we hoard them for ourselves."

Where Is Your Heart? (8–12 minutes)

Hand out Bibles and ask a volunteer to read aloud Matthew 6:19-21 as the others follow along. Then ask: "What do you think Jesus means when he says, 'Where your treasure is, there your heart will be also'?"

Say: "All of us have treasures: our time, money, and talents. Let's look at how we use these treasures in a typical week."

Distribute the How I Use My Resources handout from page 51. Ask the youth to complete the activity individually. Then have them pair off and discuss their answers with a partner.

Say: "Sit quietly and think about how you spend your time and money and what that says about your heart." Then ask:

- Is there room for God in your schedule?
- How can you use God's gifts to glorify God?
- How can you glorify God through your day-to-day activities?

OR

In Jesus' Eyes (3–5 minutes)

Ask a volunteer to read aloud Mark 12:38-44 as the others follow along. Say: "Jesus was sitting in the temple when he noticed a poor widow placing two copper coins in the offering. What she gave was less than the value of a penny today. Still, Jesus told his disciples that this poor widow gave a gift far greater the contributions of wealthy persons who gave 'out of their abundance.'" Then ask:

- What is Jesus trying to say about the large offerings of the rich people?
- How is it that the poor widow gives more than the wealthy contributors when it is obvious that she gives less?
- What does this passage say about how God feels about our gifts?
- What does this story say about the relationship between our money, our heart, and our faith?

Joyful Giving (8–13 minutes)

Ask the youth to close their eyes and place themselves in this parable as you read it to them:

Leader's Guide

the bible says ...

Provide Bibles, copies of the How I Use My Resources handout from page 51, and pens or pencils.

4

Provide Bibles.

If you plan well in advance you might be able to find actual "widow's mites" at a coin shop or online. (Try eBay.) Expect to pay $5–$10 for each.

7

go in peace

Provide student journals and pens.

In a strange land and a strange time, a decree went out to all the people from the "One In Charge." The decree was prominently posted and publicly proclaimed so that all became aware of it. The decree consisted of three words: "GIVING IS PROHIBITED!"

At first, great rejoicing was heard throughout the land. Many felt an enormous burden had been wonderfully lifted from their shoulders. They began to calculate how much happier they would surely be if they could now spend all their income and all their time on themselves and on their own needs and pleasures.

And then, strange things began to happen in this strange land and strange time. A little boy forgot the decree and picked a bouquet of flowers to give to his mother. His mother, though, was forbidden to accept them, and the flowers wound up in the trash can. A passing motorist saw a battered victim of highway robbers lying in a ditch by the road. She pulled alongside him to help, then thought better of it. "How can I help him," she said to herself, "since he obviously has nothing left with which to repay me?" And the motorist drove away, sadly.

But strangest of all were the experiences of those who rejoiced so enthusiastically when the burden of giving had been taken from them. They now found themselves no better off than before. That slim amount of income which they had been giving away was disappearing into an extra suit of clothes or a trip to an exotic land. But none of this made anyone any happier. There were still so many things just beyond reach.

A delegation was sent to the One In Charge. "We appreciate your intentions," said the spokesperson, "in lifting from us the burden of giving. But, alas, now we're doubly miserable. Not only are we frustrated that we never seem to have enough, but we've also been stripped of the joy that comes in sharing we've learned the lesson that giving is not a burden but a joy. Give back to us our joy!"[1]

Ask: "What does parable say about giving?"

Hand out student journals and ask youth to complete the activities on pages 20–23.

AND

A Fragrance to God (4–6 minutes)

Provide a candle and scented candles or potpourri.

Invite the youth to gather in a circle, and place a candle in the middle. Light scented candles, incense, or potpourri. Say: "Ephesians 5:2 describes Jesus' sacrifice as a fragrant offering to God. In the same way, we are challenged to be a fragrant offering to God, to see that our life is pleasing to God like a pleasant fragrance. As we close, let our prayer rise to God as the fragrance reminds of using our life for God. I invite you each to pray aloud ways that you intend to offer your life to God this week by giving to others of your time, money, or talents."

Allow each person to pray aloud. Close by singing the song "Sanctuary."

[1]From "Joyful Giving" by David Polk, in *The Journal of Stewardship,* Volume. 47, 1995; page 49.

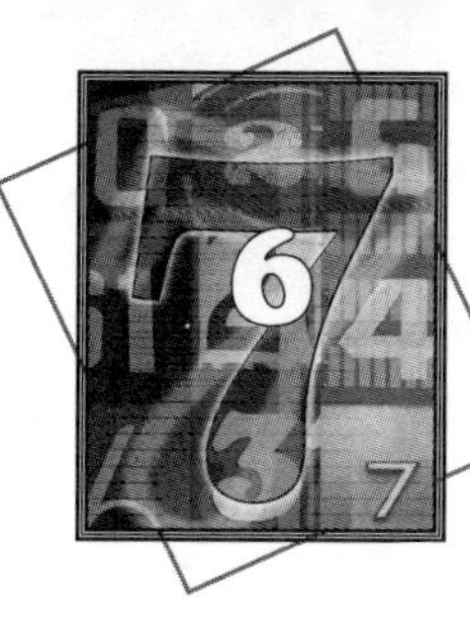

Do I Have to Share My Faith?

Topic: Being a Witness of One's Faith

Scripture: Matthew 28:19-20a; Mark 16:15; Luke 24:47-48; John 20:21; 1 Peter 3:15

Key Verse: "Repentance and forgiveness of sins is to be proclaimed in his name to all nations, beginning from Jerusalem. You are witnesses of these things" (Luke 24:47-48).

Take-Home Learning: Christians live a life of witness and are ready to tell others about the faith and hope they have found in Christ.

Younger Youth and the Topic

Many Christians find it difficult to tell others about Jesus. Some youth don't want to start the conversation if they don't have all the answers ready. Others fear ridicule or being accused of not "practicing what they preach." Still others are not sure they know the right words to use in sharing their faith. For most youth, telling others about their faith and their feelings about God is very personal and emotional, and humans are often hesitant to get emotional around people they don't know very well.

Help your youth understand that telling others about Jesus is part of faithful discipleship but at the same time honestly acknowledge their fears and concerns. Explain that witnessing is not only about talking to people. It also involves about living a life that is consistent with one's faith.

Youth may need your help in thinking both about their relationship with Jesus Christ and about how to communicate their experience. Many youth have no trouble talking endlessly about their lives—and that's most of what witnessing is: talking about one's life in Christ. You can ease their anxiety by setting a good example. Talk about your faith and how you try to live in a manner that is consistent with your faith. Remind them that no one is perfect, and that even the most confident Christians get nervous or make mistakes from time to time. Help your youth think of tangible ways to witness such as wearing symbolic clothing or jewelry or introducing a friend to a Christian recording artist. Also take give these youth an opportunity to practice verbalizing their faith in a safe environment.

Most Christians decide to live as fully devoted disciples before the age of 15. The church should not only put a great deal of effort into nurturing young disciples, but it also must train youth to be witnesses within their own culture.

Theology and the Topic

It has been said that, "The best sermon is the one lived." There is no better way to be a witness for Jesus Christ than to live as Jesus lived. Yet

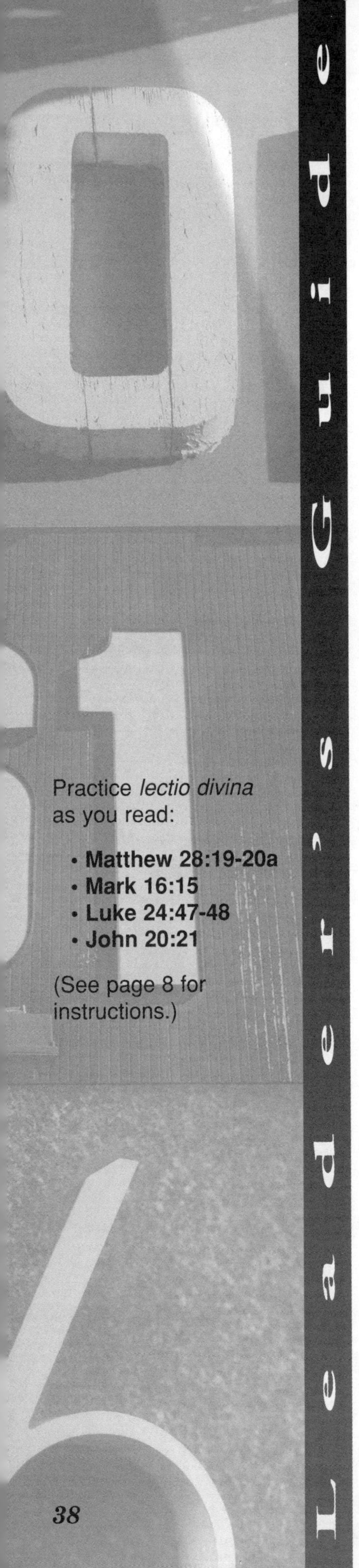

Christians are often reluctant to speak about their faith. In fact, many people are far more willing to discuss their political opinions, sex life, financial status, and mental health with others than they are willing to discuss their faith.

This is unfortunate, as the call to witness is very clear in Scripture. The Old Testament prophets are excellent examples of witnesses, proclaiming both God's warning and God's grace and favor. Jesus (who has no reservations about sharing his faith) commands his disciples to "make disciples of all nations, baptizing them in the name of the Father and of the Son and of the Holy Spirit, and teaching them to obey everything that I have commanded you" (Matthew 28:19-20a). Peter encourages the early church to "be ready to make your defense to anyone who demands from you an accounting for the hope that is in you" (1 Peter 3:15). It is also Peter who boldly proclaims the good news at Pentecost, and thousands hear and believe. The women run from the empty tomb to tell the disciples the good news of the Resurrection. The woman at the well returns to the village to tell others about her encounter with Jesus. These are but a few examples.

These stories remind us while faith is personal, it is not intended to be private. If we have really experienced the transforming power of God in our lives, we should want others to have that same emotion and experience.

You and the Scripture

Practice *lectio divina* as you read:

- **Matthew 28:19-20a**
- **Mark 16:15**
- **Luke 24:47-48**
- **John 20:21**

(See page 8 for instructions.)

As you read the four Gospel accounts of Jesus commanding the disciples to be witnesses of what they have seen and heard, consider what witnessing means to you personally.

- Are you excited by the prospect of being sent out to tell good news?
- How have you allowed the Holy Spirit to make you a more effective witness to others?
- Are you hesitant to talk about your faith? Would you rather just show your faith by the way you live?
- Think about when you were a youth. How easy was it for you to talk about your relationship with God? What could you have done better? When did you refrain from witnessing?
- How is your life today an example today of the hope that is within you?

Reflect on these questions and ask God to be with you and your youth as they learn how to be bold witnesses of Jesus Christ.

Do I Have to Share My Faith?

Scripture: Matthew 28:19-20a; Mark 16:15; Luke 24:47-48; John 20:21; 1 Peter 3:15

Take-Home Learning: Christians live a life of witness and are ready to tell others about the faith and hope they have found in Christ.

 indicates key activity. If time is limited, focus here.

activity	time	preparation	supplies
get ready			
Good News Travels Fast	5–7 minutes	Prepare five large sheets of paper according to the instructions on page 40.	Five large sheets of paper and markers
the church says . . .			
Tell Me a Story (key activity)	9–15 minutes	No preparation	Student journals and pens (A markerboard or large sheet of paper and a marker are optional.)
the bible says . . .			
Sharing the Good News (key activity)	13–15 minutes	Duplicate the Sharing the Good News handout from page 52.	Bibles, handouts, and pens or pencils
AND			
Speak Up (key activity)	12–15 minutes	Duplicate the Speak Up! Case Studies from page 53.	Handouts
go in peace			
Pop Quiz	4–7 minutes	Review the acronyms on page 42.	Paper, pens or pencils, a markerboard or large sheet of paper, and a marker
AND			
They'll Know We Are Christians	4–6 minutes	No preparation	A candle and hymnals or songbooks including the song, "They'll Know We Are Christians by Our Love"

get ready

Provide five large sheets of paper, and markers.

the church says ...

Provide student journals and pens. A markerboard or large sheet of paper and a marker are optional.

Leader's Guide

Good News Travels Fast (5–7 minutes)

Beforehand, post five large sheets of paper, one with each of the following titles:

- Ways we communicate news or events of the day
- Things that have to be shared with someone else
- Personal things that are never shared with others
- Topics of conversation between you and your friends
- Topics that you and your friends would never talk about

As the youth arrive, encourage them to take a marker and to write examples on each of the sheets. Encourage them to list as many examples as they can.

When everyone has arrived, look over the answers on each sheet. Read aloud each example, then ask the youth if they see any trends or notice any items on more than one list. Help the youth draw conclusions from their answers. Then ask:

- What about faith? Is faith a personal and private matter, or is it something we should talk about?
- Can faith be personal without being private? Explain.
- Why is it sometimes difficult for Christians to share our faith with others?

Say: "Today's session is on witnessing. Living the Christian life involves telling others about our faith and our experience with Jesus Christ. This can be difficult, but it can also strengthen our faith."

Ask: "How would you define 'witnessing'?"

Explain that witnessing simply means telling others what you have experienced. Just as courtroom witnesses tell of their experiences at the scene of the crime, Christians should tells others of their experiences with God's grace.

Tell Me a Story (9–15 minutes)

Divide the group into pairs. (Try to separate best friends.) Say: "You and your partner will take turns telling each other stories. The younger person will go first. Tell a story about one of these subjects":

- A family vacation or trip
- A meaningful holiday or celebration
- An individual who is very important to you
- A time you accomplished something you were very proud of

(You might want to list these subjects on a markerboard or large sheet of paper.)

Give the pairs about five minutes to exchange stories. Then ask:

- How difficult was it to tell someone a story about your life?
- Why do you think it is that so many of our conversations involve telling stories?
- Why do we sometimes refer to our Christian journey as our "faith story"?
- Would you say it is easy or hard for for most people you know to tell their faith stories to others?

Say: "Sometimes it's easier for us to talk about our faith when we realize that all we have to do is tell a story. Witnessing doesn't always mean quoting Bible verses or making deep theological arguments. Often it just means telling a true story that can touch other people. We're going to spend a few minutes thinking about some of the faith stories we might tell others."

Hand out student journals and give youth about four minutes to complete the activities on pages 24–27.

Sharing the Good News (13–15 minutes)

Hand out Bibles and the Sharing the Good News handout from page 52. Divide the youth into three groups and assign each group one of the three sections. Ask the groups to read aloud the Scriptures and to discuss their answers to the questions. Give the groups about ten minutes to work then have a spokesperson from each group summarize its discussion. Bring the activity to a close by reviewing and summarizing what you heard from each of the groups.

AND

Speak Up (12–15 minutes)

Distribute copies of the Speak Up! Case Studies from page 53. Say: "Think about how you talk when you are around non-Christians. What do you talk about? What subjects do you avoid? Do you think people can tell from your conversations that you are a Christian? When we mention God or talk with excitement about the role of Jesus in our lives, we invite others to think about their spiritual lives."

Say: "Let's look at some situations where we could witness to others." Divide the youth into groups of three. Tell each group to select three case studies from the handout to roleplay. In each situation a Christian friend (or friends) will have an opportunity to tell his or her faith story or to talk about how God is at work in our lives.

Give the groups plenty of time to roleplay the scenarios. Then bring the youth back together and allow volunteers to report what they learned from this activity.

the bible says ...

Provide Bibles, copies of the Sharing the Good News handout from page 52, and pens or pencils.

If you are working with a large number of youth, divide them into six groups and have two groups work on each section.

Provide copies of the Speak Up! Case Studies from page 53.

go in peace

Provide paper, pens or pencils, a markerboard or large sheet of paper, and a marker.

Explain that an acronym is a word created using the first letters of other words.

Pop Quiz (4–7 minutes)

Give each youth a sheet of paper. Write on a markerboard or large sheet of paper the acronyms I.B.N.O., W.W.J.D., and F.R.O.G. Ask the youth to copy these onto their sheet of paper.

Say: "It's time for a pop quiz. You have one minute to write down what you think these letters stand for."

Give the youth exactly a minute then ask volunteers to tell their answers. Then give them the correct answers.

- **I.B.N.O.:** In But Not Of (the crowd or the world)
- **W.W.J.D.:** What Would Jesus Do?
- **F.R.O.G.:** Fully Rely On God

Say: "These acronyms stand for the three imperatives, or things we must do, in Christian witnessing." (Although these are the correct answers, other answers are not necessarily wrong. Commend youth who come up with creative answers that are still relevant to the subject of Christian witness.) Then ask:

- How did you feel when I announced we were having a pop quiz? How do you feel when one of your school teachers announces a pop quiz?
- How are your feelings about taking a pop quiz similar to your feelings when someone asks you about your faith in Jesus Christ?
- What does each of these three acronyms have to do with sharing your faith with others?

Say: "These three simple acronyms can help you become an effective witness to the 'hope that is within you.'"

OR

Provide a candle and hymnals or songbooks including "They'll Know We Are Christians by Our Love."

They'll Know We Are Christians (4–6 minutes)

Gather the youth in a circle and place a lit candle in the middle. Sing at the chorus of the song, "They'll Know We Are Christians by Our Love." Then ask the youth to close their eyes for a time of silent prayer. Invite the youth to ask God to make them aware of someone who needs to hear about God's love through Jesus Christ. Go around the circle and have the youth say their relationship to that person. (For example, "my friend," "my classmate," or "someone in my family.") Then have the youth pray silently, asking God for guidance as they witness to these persons.

Close by praying aloud, asking God to guide the youth this week as they seek to witness to the hope that is within them.

How Will I Know What God Is Calling Me to Do?

Topic: Using One's Spiritual Gifts

Scripture: 1 Samuel 3:1-11; Isaiah 6:1-8; Matthew 4:18-22; Romans 12:3-8; 1 Corinthians 12:4-11, 28; Galatians 5:22-26; Ephesians 4:7-14

Key Verse: "And he said to them, 'Follow me, and I will make you fish for people'" (Matthew 4:19).

Take-Home Learning: We can know the will of God by the gifts we have received.

Younger Youth and the Topic

Youth want to make a difference in the world. They want their lives to have meaning and purpose, and they want to do what they do well. Many young adolescents try a little bit of everything, uncertain of where their talents lie. And, like many adults, they often underestimate their own abilities.

The adolescent years are crucial in shaping a person's identity. As youth, many persons get a sense of what careers they are suited for and begin to specialize. Too often, however, youth do not see ministry in their future. Though ordained ministry is not for everyone, youth need to understand that they can be ministers without wearing a stole or standing at the pulpit. As Christians, we are all called to be ministers, regardless of our profession. The church should help younger youth get a sense of who they are, what they desire, what their gifts and graces are, and how they can play a part in God's ongoing work.

Theology and the Topic

Author Stephen Bryant writes, "Spiritual discernment makes operational our faith that an ever present Guide . . . is present to lead us in the way of truth and love."[1] The Bible contains wonderful and dramatic stories of people who seek God's will above all else. Moses learned of God's will for his life when God spoke to him through the burning bush (Exodus 3:1—4:17). Jacob felt God's continued presence as he fought with an angel in the night (Genesis 32:22-32). God called the young boy Samuel directly (1 Samuel 3:1-11). And when God sent Samuel to select one of Jesse's sons to be King, God led Samuel to recognize the heart of David by saying, "The Lord does not see as mortals see; they look on the outward appearance, but the Lord looks on the heart" (1 Samuel 16:1-13). Elijah

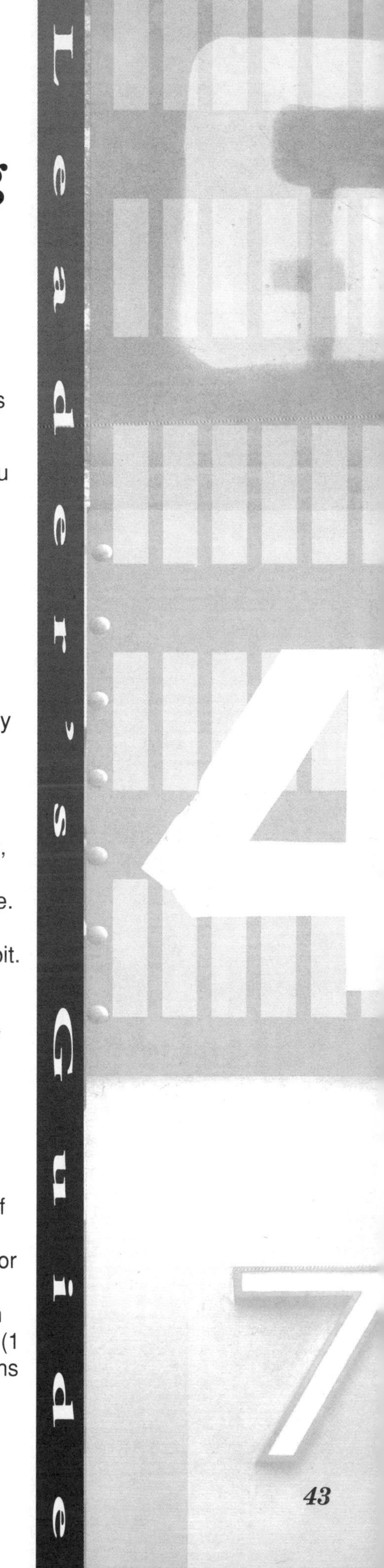

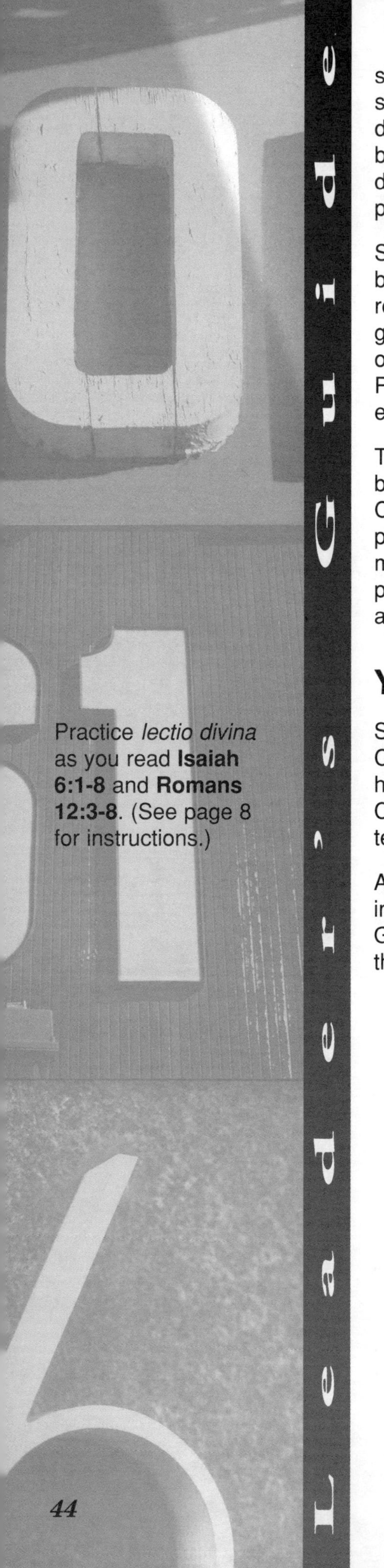

stood in the entrance to a cave and found God in the sound of sheer silence (1 Kings 19:11-12). In Romans Paul mentions spiritual discernment directly when he writes, "Do not be conformed to this world, but be transformed by the renewing of your minds, so that you may discern what is the will of God—what is good and acceptable and perfect" (Romans 12:2).

Since its early years, the church has sought to discern the will of God both individually and communally. Spiritual discernment involves recognizing the gifts one has been given and learning how to use these gifts according to God's will. In fact our gifts are an indication of the will of God in our lives and of our call to discipleship. In Romans 12:3-8, Paul explains the holy life, using images of a human body to show that each of us has an important and useful task to do.

The body is representative of the church. Just as parts of the human body must work together if the body is going to function properly, Christians must work together in harmony if the church is to function properly. As the church is made up of many types of people, there are many types of gifts. Some have been called to preach, others to teach, prophecy, heal, feed, or clothe. Some specialize in leadership and administration. Each of these roles is vital to the life of the church.

You and the Scripture

Practice *lectio divina* as you read **Isaiah 6:1-8** and **Romans 12:3-8**. (See page 8 for instructions.)

Spend some quiet moments in prayer, meditation, and reflection. Consider how God is using you to build up the faith of your youth and how God has called you to teach them these basics of living the Christian faith. What gifts God has given you that will help you as you teach?

As you prepare for this lesson, make a list of your gifts, talents, and interests. Think about what you bring to the life of the church. Pray that God will help you continue to identify and develop your spiritual gifts and that God will show you how to use your gifts for the good of the church.

How Will I Know What God Is Calling Me to Do?

Scripture: 1 Samuel 3:1-11; Isaiah 6:1-8; Matthew 4:18-22; Romans 12:3-8; 1 Corinthians 12:4-11, 28; Galatians 5:22-26; Ephesians 4:7-14

Take-Home Learning: We can know the will of God by the gifts we have received.

 indicates key activity. If time is limited, focus here.

activity	time	preparation	supplies
get ready			
Careers in the Cartoons (key activity)	7–12 minutes	Gather books of popular comic strips or comic pages from recent newspapers.	Books of popular comic strips, comic pages from recent newspapers, sticky notes, and pens or pencils
the church says ...			
Job Listing (key activity)	6–12 minutes	Collect job listings from recent newspapers.	Newspaper job listings, large sheets of paper, markers, and a markerboard (optional)
the bible says ...			
Gifts for Living (key activity)	15–25 minutes	Duplicate the survey from pages 54–56.	Bibles, surveys, pens or pencils, a markerboard or large sheet of paper, and a marker
AND			
Come With Me	4–7 minutes	Arrange for someone to call you out of the room after you read aloud the Scripture.	No supplies
go in peace			
Gifts of the Spirit	11–13 minutes	Review Galatians 5:22-26.	Bibles, student journals, and pens
OR			
A Call to Discipleship	4–7 minutes	No preparation	A candle and hymnals or songbooks

get ready

Provide books of popular comic strips that deal with work or comic pages from recent newspapers, sticky notes, and pens or pencils.

Careers in the Cartoons (7–12 minutes)

Beforehand, gather books of popular comic strips, especially comic strips that frequently deal with work. (The library would be a good place to start.) You might also use the comic pages of recent newspapers.

As youth arrive, hand a book or page of comics to each youth. (If you have a large number of youth, divide the youth into pairs or small groups.) Give each youth sticky notes to mark pages. Say: "Find comic strips that deal with jobs and working. Find as many as you can and mark the pages with sticky notes. Jot down on the sticky notes what attitude each comic strip takes toward work."

Give the youth a few minutes to browse the comics, then ask volunteers to report what attitudes were at play. Then ask:

- Why do you think so many cartoons poke fun at work or work situations?
- When adults meet someone new, one of the first questions they usually ask is, "What do you do?" Why is work something people talk about so much?
- Do you think most people are happy at their jobs? Why or why not? Do you think you'll be happy in your first long-term job? Why or why not?
- Why are some persons more likely to be happy with their job?

the church says ...

Provide newspaper job listings (one page for every two or three youth), a markerboard or large sheet of paper, large sheets of paper (one for every two or three youth), and markers.

Job Listing (6–12 minutes)

Beforehand, divide a markerboard or large sheet of paper into two columns. Label the first column, "Jobs," and the second column, "Talents, Skills, Interests, Values, and Personality Traits Needed." Use a job that you are familiar with (perhaps your own job) as an example.

Divide the youth into groups of two or three. Give each group a page of job listings from the local newspaper, a large sheet of paper, and markers. Tell the groups to make a chart similar to the one you've created. Then ask each group to select four jobs advertised in the paper and to fill out their chart for these jobs. In addition to jobs they find in the paper, ask each group to include two or three church-related positions on their chart. Point out your example, and encourage them to list as many items as possible in the second column.

Give the groups about five minutes to work, then have each group tell about one job it found in the paper and one church-related job. Add these jobs to your chart. Then ask:

- Which of these jobs could you never imagine yourself doing? Why are these jobs so unappealing?
- Why might someone be extremely unhappy with the work he or she is doing?

- If a person sees his or her skills or talents as gifts from God, how might that change his or her approach to work? What is the difference between seeing work as a job and seeing work as a calling?
- What if a person were unable to find a job doing what he or she felt called to do?

Gifts for Living (15–25 minutes)

Hand out Bibles. Ask for volunteers to read aloud Romans 12:3-8, 1 Corinthians 12:4-11, 28, and Ephesians 4:7-14 as others follow along. After each passage has been read, ask youth to name the gifts mentioned in the Scripture that are given to the church or that build up the church. List these on a markerboard or large sheet of paper.

Then distribute copies of the survey from pages 54–56. Allow time for youth to complete all three pages, except for the questions on the bottom of Discovering My Values. When they have finished, instruct them to write a paragraph on the back of one of the pages describing their qualities. For example, "I am a unique person," "I enjoy learning," or "I need to feel respected."

When youth have finished writing their paragraphs, tell them to answer the questions at the bottom of the Discovering My Values page.

Invite volunteers to read aloud their descriptive paragraphs or how they answered the questions on the survey. Affirm their work and make sure the youth are respectful of one another's conclusions.

Say: "God has given each of us gifts. When we use these gifts to do God's work, we fill our lives with meaning and purpose. Some of you may feel like you have a clear sense God's call, while others of you may still be listening. Either way, look for opportunities to use and develop the gifts you've been given. We have a responsibility to share what God has given us with the church and with the world."

the bible says ...

Provide Bibles, copies of the survey from pages 54–56, pens or pencils, and a markerboard or large sheet of paper, and a marker

AND

Come With Me (4–7 minutes)

Before class, arrange for someone to call you out of the room immediately after you have read aloud Matthew 4:18-22. Ask the person to say, "You need to come with me. Leave what are you doing and come now," in a firm voice.

Read aloud the Scripture. When you are asked to leave the room, immediately leave the room without comment. Stay out of the room a full two minutes before returning. When you return, ask:

- What did you think was happening when I was called from the room?

You may need to give the person who is calling you a signal so he or she will know when to interrupt the class.

- Would following Jesus ever require you to pick up and leave everything behind immediately?
- Why do you think Jesus chose fishermen to be his first followers? Do you think Simon, Andrew, James, and John believed they had all of the talents and gifts they needed to 'fish for people'?

go in peace

Provide Bibles, student journals, and pens.

Gifts of the Spirit (11–13 minutes)

Ask the youth to read in unison Galatians 5:22-26. Say: "To live according to God's will is to reflect the fruit of the Spirit regardless of what we are called to do."

Tell the youth that you're going to read the passage again. Ask them to close their eyes and to listen for one word or phrase that grabs their attention. Slowly re-read aloud Galatians 5:22-26.

Ask volunteers to say what word or phrase attracted their attention. Then ask: "How can we know that we are doing the will of God?" (*Possible answer: We will see evidence of love, joy, peace, patience, kindness, generosity, faithfulness, gentleness, and self-control.*)

Hand out student journals and allow youth about five minutes to silently complete the activities on pages 28–31. If time permits, have youth pair off and discuss their answers to the questions in the student journal.

Close by praying for guidance as you continue to identify your gifts and learn how to use them to do God's will.

OR

Provide a candle and hymnals or songbooks including "I Have Decided to Follow Jesus," or "They'll Know We Are Christians by Our Love."

A Call To Discipleship (4–7 minutes)

Gather youth in a circle and place a lit candle in the middle. Pray for guidance as you continue to identify your gifts and learn how to use them to do God's will.

Then close by singing "I Have Decided to Follow Jesus" or "They'll Know We Are Christians by Our Love."

[1]From "What Is Spiritual Discernment by Consensus?" by Stephen Bryant, in *Raising Prayer to a Lifestyle*, Volume 2, Issue 1, July–September 1994; page 2.

Choices—A Case Study

Aaron is the starting point guard for his school's basketball team. Next Friday is the big game against his school's arch rival. The game had originally been scheduled for a Tuesday but was postponed due to bad weather. Aaron's youth group has been planning a ski retreat for several months which now will take place the same weekend as the game. The youth group will be leaving immediately after school next Friday and driving three hours to the retreat location.

If Aaron doesn't go to the game, his teammates will be very angry, and the coach may make him sit out the rest of the season. However, Aaron's parents are chaperones for the ski trip and are committed to going with the youth group after school. If he doesn't go on the retreat, he will have to stay with his grandparents for the entire weekend, missing all of the fun he would have had on the ski trip.

Characters:

- **Aaron**
- **Aaron's coach**
- **Aaron's youth leader**
- **Teammate #1** (understands Aaron's dilemma)
- **Teammate #2** (can't understand why Aaron would want to miss the game for a church activity)
- **Youth group friend #1** (understands Aaron's dilemma)
- **Youth group friend #2** (can't understand why Aaron would want to miss the ski trip for a basketball game)

Roleplay conversations between Aaron and his coach, Aaron and his teammates, Aaron and his youth leader, and Aaron and his youth group friends.

Then discuss these questions that are helpful in making decisions:

- How will Aaron feel if he stays home and plays in the game?
- How will Aaron feel if he goes on the retreat but misses the game?
- What compromises could Aaron make in this situation?
- What are the consequences of each decision?
- What's the best thing that could possibly happen?
- What's the worst thing that could possibly happen?
- How will Aaron's decision affect others? How should this affect the choice he makes?
- Have you ever been in a situation like Aaron's? What did you do? Looking back, do you think you made the right choice? Would you want to make that decision again?

Whose Job Is It?

Look at these jobs and tasks, and decide who should be responsible for each one. Answer using the code below. You may have more than one answer for each item.

M=Me **P=Parents** **A=Another Adult** **S=Someone else**

- Pick up trash on roads, streets, and highways
- Recycle the family's soft-drink cans and newspapers
- Work at a soup kitchen
- Turn the lights out when leaving a room
- Take at least one shower or bath every day
- Drive to school events
- Do the laundry
- Take out the trash
- Use environmentally safe cleaning products and biodegradable plastics
- Plant trees
- Volunteer to be a peer mediator or tutor
- Visit shut-ins
- Work on a Habitat for Humanity house
- Write letters to elected representatives about issues like pollution and poverty
- Make healthy lifestyle choices
- Tell a friend about Jesus
- Visit someone who is sick
- Do yard work for a neighbor who is unable to do it

Session 4 Reproducible Page

How I Use My Resources

Fill in all of your week's activities on the calendar below. You may use abbreviations like "Sch" for "School" and "HW" for Homework. Include spending time with your friends, going shopping, and other non-scheduled activities. Think about which of these activities you spend money on. Below record these activities as "Expenses." Record how much money you spent on each activity as a "Cost." You may need to list your expenses and costs on a separate sheet of paper.

	Sunday	Monday	Tuesday	Wednesday	Thursday	Friday	Saturday
6 A.M.							
7 A.M.							
8 A.M.							
9 A.M.							
10 A.M.							
11 A.M.							
12 P.M.							
1 P.M.							
2 P.M.							
3 P.M.							
4 P.M.							
5 P.M.							
6 P.M.							
7 P.M.							
8 P.M.							
9 P.M.							
10 P.M.							

Expenses	Cost	Expenses	Cost

Session 5 Reproducible Page

Sharing the Good News

Group #1

Read aloud **Matthew 28:19-20a**; **Mark 16:15**; **Luke 24:47-48**; **John 20:21**.

- What does Jesus command his disciples to do when he leaves them?
- Think about how you and your Christian friends are witnesses for Jesus Christ. How does what Christians say and do bring others closer to Jesus?
- How do Christians sometimes discourage others from seeking a relationship with Christ?
- How do our actions serve as a witness? As Christ's representatives on earth, how should we act?

Group #2

Read aloud **1 Corinthians 9:22**; **1 Peter 2:11-16**; **3:15**.

- According to these Scriptures, how are we to witness to others?
- How do you think Christianity is viewed by most non-Christians? Why?
- When do Christian teens have trouble matching their actions to their beliefs?
- How does a person's culture affect how we share the gospel with him or her?

Group #3

Read aloud **Acts 22:17-21**.

- Have you ever tried to tell someone about your faith, only to be turned away? How did you feel?
- How should Christians react when they are ignored or made fun of?
- How can you bring God's light into dark situations?
- In the Book of Jonah, Jonah rejects God's call to witness in Nineveh because he didn't think the people would change. He ran away—only to end up in the belly of a big fish. Think about those people you think will never change their ways. Who are you tempted to run away from? How can you reach out to these persons?

Speak Up! Case Studies

Case Study #1

Kyle's parents are getting a divorce. He is angry, frustrated, and confused, and he feels abandoned by both his mother and his father. How could you share God's love with Kyle? How could God's love help Kyle deal with this difficult situation?

Case Study #2

Allyson tells you that she feels empty inside. Everything is OK with her life, but she feels like she is missing something. How could you tell Allyson about life with Jesus Christ? How could Christ help Allyson feel more complete?

Case Study #3

Nathan tells you about yesterday's basketball practice. His shots weren't falling and he wasn't moving his feet enough on defense. The coach was furious and had some very harsh words for him. Nathan says he feels like quitting because he is not a good player and he doesn't get along with the coach. How could you tell Nathan about the love and support you've found at church? How could this love and support help Nathan through his problems?

Session 6 Reproducible Page

Discovering My Interests

- [ ] I enjoy belonging to organizations.
- [ ] I give myself time for exercise and rest.
- [ ] I set goals for myself.
- [ ] I need to win.
- [ ] I prefer to cooperate.
- [ ] I look for new challenges.
- [ ] I always do my best.
- [ ] I enjoy preparing and eating food.
- [ ] I enjoy being male or being female.
- [ ] I need to be accepted by others.
- [ ] I am my own person.
- [ ] I want to be rewarded for success.
- [ ] I always want more stuff.
- [ ] I need to get things done.
- [ ] I am easy going.
- [ ] I stay organized.
- [ ] I enjoy learning.
- [ ] I need to know that my future is secure.
- [ ] I dislike taking risks.
- [ ] I relate well to others.
- [ ] I enjoy change.
- [ ] I like people or situations that are unique or different.
- [ ] I enjoy serving others.
- [ ] I like speaking in front of a crowd.
- [ ] I am a good listener.
- [ ] I like to teach people new things.
- [ ] I want to know exactly how things work.
- [ ] I use money responsibly.
- [ ] I am creative and enjoy making new things.
- [ ] I draw, paint, or sculpt.
- [ ] I sing or play an instrument.
- [ ] I like to travel.
- [ ] I enjoy being a part of something that is bigger than me.
- [ ] I like to be appreciated for my accomplishments.

Discovering My Talents

List ten talents or abilities that you feel that you have:

1)
2)
3)
4)
5)
6)
7)
8)
9)
10)

List ten talents or gifts that others say that you have:

1)
2)
3)
4)
5)
6)
7)
8)
9)
10)

List five talents, gifts, or abilities from above that you really enjoy having:

1)
2)
3)
4)
5)

Session 7 Reproducible Page

Discovering My Values

Check the values on this list that are important to you.

- [ ] Good family relationships
- [ ] Financial security
- [ ] Job security
- [ ] Adventure
- [ ] Strong religious faith
- [ ] Tolerance and acceptance
- [ ] Creativity
- [ ] Fame
- [ ] Good looks
- [ ] Physical fitness
- [ ] Having a set routine
- [ ] Having time to myself
- [ ] Community involvement
- [ ] Variety
- [ ] Political power
- [ ] Popularity
- [ ] Recognition
- [ ] Prestige
- [ ] Freedom from stress
- [ ] Control
- [ ] Strong friendships
- [ ] Financial success
- [ ] Freedom to live where I choose
- [ ] Leisure time
- [ ] Safety
- [ ] Comfort and luxury
- [ ] World peace
- [ ] Parenthood
- [ ] Good health
- [ ] Compassion and concern for others
- [ ] ______________________________
- [ ] ______________________________
- [ ] ______________________________
- [ ] ______________________________

- **What careers would best fit your interests, talents, and values?**

- **How can each of these careers be a ministry even if it isn't related to the church?**

- **After looking at your interests, talents, and values, do you feel called to work in the church?**

Session 7 Reproducible Page

"What's a Christian to Do?" Retreat

Theme: I Have Decided to Follow Jesus

Purpose: To help youth discover the joy of Christian living.

Preparation: Several weeks before the retreat, assemble of group of youth and adults to plan the retreat. Select one youth and one adult to co-direct the retreat and coordinate small-group planning. Plan for a weekend retreat to be held in your local church or at a nearby camp or retreat center. The facility should have electricity for viewing movies and listening to music. Also choose a setting that offers a variety of entertainment and recreation opportunities.

Determine a cost per person for the retreat. Provide registration and permission forms, and set a registration deadline. Send letters to parents detailing retreat plans and activities.

Determine rules for communal living—cleaning and cooking, sleeping arrangements, and so forth. Provide a student journal and a small notebook for each participant and remind everyone to bring a Bible.

Friday

Allow everyone time to unpack, find their way around, and unwind before dinner.

Welcome

Greet the participants and give them an overview of the schedule for the retreat. If some participants do not know one another well, plan an icebreaker or two so everyone can learn names. Then move in silence to your worship space.

Worship and Prayer: Sabbath Time

Ask one participant to read aloud Mark 6:30-32.

Say: "God rested on the seventh day. In the Jewish tradition, the Sabbath day, the day of rest, began at sundown on Friday. In the Christian tradition, Sunday is the Sabbath. Both traditions observe a time of rest during the week. An aspect of Christian living is following the example of Jesus by making time for rest and reflection."

Friday

3:00 PM Arrival, time to get settled

5:30 PM Dinner

(Foil dinners are easy to make and can involve the cooperation of many participants. They make a great meal if you have the time and resources.)

6:00 PM Welcome

6:15 PM Worship and Prayer

Hand out the small notebooks. Say: "These notebooks will be your journals for the weekend. Use your journal to record notes from our discussions and thoughts that God might bring to your mind. Some of your writings this weekend will be of use long after this retreat is finished. For your first journal entry, find a place where you can be alone and reflect about the need for Sabbath rest. Think about these questions":

- Why is rest important for good physical, mental, and spiritual health?
- Does your life ever get so busy that you miss out on Sabbath rest? If so, how can you make time for rest in the midst of your busy schedule?

Come up with a signal to let the participants know when to stop working and to return. Allow participants twenty minutes to work before giving the signal.

When everyone has returned, sing a few songs together or do some of the activities from a book of worship ideas, such as *Worship Feast: 100 Awesome Ideas for Postmodern Youth* (Abingdon Press, 2003).

7:00 PM Aspects of Christian living

Aspects of Christian Living: Covenant

Divide the youth into two or more groups to read and discuss Genesis 9:1-7. Say: "This Scripture is about God's covenant with Noah. A covenant is like a contract in which two or more parties all agree to do something for one another." Ask the groups to determine the purpose of the covenant, the responsibility of each party involved, and the sign of the covenant. (*God will give humankind dominion over creation. Humankind is to avoid eating flesh with blood or shedding the blood of another person, and to be "fruitful and multiply."*)

Then have each participant make a covenant with God concerning the care of creation including the earth, themselves, and other persons. Ask them be specific about how they will take responsibility environment, themselves, and others. Invite volunteers to present their covenants.

7:30 PM Nighttime scavenger hunt

This scavenger hunt will be more interesting if you ask youth to keep track of their findings with a digital camera or video camera.

Nighttime Scavenger Hunt

An environmental scavenger hunt is one way to explore and enjoy creation. Send both youth and adults, as individuals or in small groups, to find items on a list, giving them the instruction that they must not destroy any part of creation to gather the items on the list. Suggested items are listed below.

- A non-living thing that never was alive
- A non-living thing that once was alive
- An animal that is not an insect
- Something from under a rock

- Ten different types of leaves (watch out for poison ivy)
- Something an animal would eat
- Something that you wish were not in this environment
- Something that you're glad is in this environment

Come back and celebrate everyone's finds. If you'd like, award one point for each item found and declare a winner. Provide a small prize for the winning individual or team. Return any living creatures to their natural environments.

Movie: *Pay It Forward*

Pop some popcorn (over a fire if possible) and settle down to watch *Pay it Forward* on DVD or VHS. Be sure to read the note on permissions on page 61. Since this movie is rated PG-13 and contains some potentially objectionable content, be sure to get permission from each youth's parents. You will discuss the movie on Saturday.

9:00 PM Movie

Provide a VCR or DVD player and a television.

11:30 PM Lights out

Saturday

Morning Devotion

After breakfast, have a brief "Morning Watch" together. Create your own worship service or devotional, use worship or devotional ideas from a book, or assign one session in the student journal. Also invite youth to record their thoughts on yesterday's activities in their notebooks.

Saturday

7:00 AM Wake up

8:00 AM Breakfast

8:45 AM Morning Devotion

Aspects of Christian Living: Going to Church

Do the following activities from Session 1 (Do I Have to Go to Church?):

- Top Ten Reasons to Go to Church (page 10)
- Instruction for Living (page 10)

Then give the youth time to enjoy the retreat setting until lunch. You may plan some group games or activities.

9:30 AM Aspects of Christian Living

10:30 AM Free Time

12:00 PM Lunch

Nature Walk: A Time for Silence and Reflection

After lunch give participants some time to rest. Then take a nature walk together. Instruct the youth to walk in silence. However, allow youth to stop the group at any time by pointing out something they feel is especially beautiful or spiritual or that reminds them of God.

12:45 Nature Walk

1:45 PM Aspects of Christian Living

3:00 PM Free Time

4:30 PM Afternoon Devotion

5:00 PM Dinner

5:45 PM Games and Recreation

Go For It! (Abingdon Press, 1998) includes a number of suggestions for noncompetitive, cooperative games.

7:00 PM Aspects of Christian Living

8:30 PM Break and Snacks

9:00 PM Movie

Provide a VCR or DVD player and a television.

11:00 PM Lights Out

Leader's Guide

Aspects of Christian Living: Stewardship

Discuss the movie *Pay It Forward*. Talk about how characters in the movie use their time, money, and talent to change their world for the better. Use the questions on page 23 of the student journal to guide your discussion. Ask: "Does this movie provide an example we can all follow?" Then have volunteers rate the movie using stars: ★★★★ is excellent; ★ is poor.

Afternoon Devotion

Create your own devotional or brief worship service or use worship or devotional ideas from a book. Give participants an opportunity to say where they have seen or heard God on the retreat so far. Also invite youth to record their thoughts on yesterday's activities in their notebooks.

Games and Recreation

Play some noncompetitive, cooperative games. Talk briefly with the youth about the good and bad aspects of competition and how cooperation is important to the body of Christ.

Aspects of Christian Living: Witnessing

Do the following activities from Session Six, "Do I Have to Share My Faith?":

- Good News Travels Fast (page 40)
- Tell Me a Story (page 40)
- Sharing the Good News (page 41)

Movie: *Simon Birch*

Break out the snacks and settle in for a viewing of the movie, *Simon Birch* on VHS or DVD. Ask the group to think about God's call as they watch the movie. Since this movie contains some potentially objectionable content, be sure to get permission from each youth's parents. You will discuss the movie on Sunday.

Sunday

Aspects of Christian Living: Discernment

Do the following activities from Session Two (How Do I Pray Without Ceasing?):

- What is Prayer? (page 16)
- Instruction for Living (page 16)
- Meeting God in Everyday Life (page 17)

Aspects of Christian Living: Calling

Break into small groups of about five people. Ask them to answer the following questions:

- What do you think of when you hear words like 'call' or 'calling'?
- When have you felt God's call in your life?
- How do you think God is calling you today?

Discuss the movie *Simon Birch* with these questions in mind. Then break for lunch.

After lunch, do the following activities from Session Seven (How Will I Know What God Is Calling Me to Do?):

- Job Listing (page 46)
- Gifts for Living (page 47)

Then ask:

- How has this weekend changed your understanding of what God is calling you to do?
- As a group, how can we become more faithful to God's call in our lives?

Closing Worship

Close with Worship Service: The Summons from pages 63–64.

Notes on Video Viewing:

When you show home videocassettes or DVDs to a group of learners, you need to obtain a license. You can get a public performance license (sometimes called a site or umbrella license) from The Motion Picture Licensing Corporation's church desk at 800-515-8855. The license is valid for twelve months and typically costs about $95. Check with your church to see if an umbrella license has already been obtained. Many denominations—through conferences, jurisdictions, dioceses, and other structures—secure licenses for their churches.

Leader's Guide

Sunday

7:00 AM Rise

8:00 AM Breakfast

9:00 AM Aspects of Christian Living

10:30 AM Break

11:00 AM Aspects of Christian Living

12:15 PM Lunch

12:45 PM Aspects of Christian Living

1:45 PM Clean up and pack

2:30 PM Closing Worship

7

Out and About: Extend Each Session

Here are a few suggestions for extending each session or trying something different during the Sunday school hour:

Session One: Participating in Church

- Visit a worship service help by another denomination or faith tradition.
- Invite members of your church to talk about the importance of the church in their lives.

Session Two: Praying

- Invite members of your church to talk about how and where they pray and about the importance of prayer to their Christian walk.
- Visit a church in your community that has a labyrinth.

Session Three: Connecting With God in All Things

- Invite a trained Spiritual Director to do Group Spiritual Direction with your youth. (See www.shalem.org for more details.)
- Spend a day searching for God in silence, prayer, service, worship, Scripture, community, and everyday life. Have youth record their experiences for use in worship.

Session Four: Caring for Creation

- Do yard work for a shut-in or volunteer, clean up a city park, or spend a day working at a Habitat for Humanity site.

Session Five: Using Time, Talent, and Money for God

- Invite members of the church (or staff who deal with finances) to talk about stewardship and tithing.

Session Six: Telling Others the Good News

- Share your faith by visiting a youth home or juvenile detention center.

Session Seven: Hearing God's Call

- Invite a career counselor to administer aptitude tests and talk with youth about vocations and careers.
- Invite a clergyperson to talk about his or her call to ordained ministry.

Worship Service: The Summons

Provide copies of the Prayers handout from page 64 and copies of The Faith We Sing *or another praise and worship songbook.*

Welcome and Opening Prayer

Open by reading aloud John 1:43-51. Say: "Just as Jesus called Philip and Nathanael, he summons each of us today."

Then sing "Sanctuary." (It can be found in most praise and worship songbooks.)

Invite participants to bow their heads in prayer. Pray in unison the Opening Prayer from the Prayers handout.

Sing "The Summons" (2130 in *The Faith We Sing*) as a hymn of invitation.

Confession

Pray the Prayer of Confession from the Prayers handout.

Then sing "Change My Heart, O God" (2152 in *The Faith We Sing*) as a response.

Sharing the Good News

Say: "Jesus, undeterred, went right ahead and gave his charge: 'God authorized and commanded me to commission you: Go out and train everyone you meet, far and near, in this way of life, marking them by baptism in the threefold name: Father, Son, and Holy Spirit. Then instruct them in the practice of all I have commanded you. I'll be with you as you do this, day after day after day, right up to the end of the age'" (Matthew 28:18-20, *The Message*).

Then invite youth to say what living the Christian life means to them.

Sing "I Have Decided to Follow Jesus" (2129 in *The Faith We Sing*).

Holy Communion

If a clergyperson is present to bless the elements, offer Holy Communion.

Benediction

Say: "Jesus said to his disciples before he left them, 'You're the witnesses. What comes next is very important: I am sending what my Father promised to you, so stay here in the city until he arrives, until you're equipped with power from on high'" (Luke 24:48-49, *The Message*).

Prayers

Opening Prayer

(*Read in unison.*)

God, you have found a place in our lives. We welcome you. Yet we are still learning how you want us to live. We want to be faithful in our living, in our serving, in our giving, in our loving. We want to follow you. Yet we are not sure of the way. Prepare our lives so that you will always find a welcoming home in us and us in you. We thank you, God, for our journey. Help us to be like Christ, so that others may know you through us. Amen.

Prayer of Confession

(*Pause for a moment of silence after each statement.*)

God, we have not been quiet enough to hear your call. (*silence*)

God, we have not joined in the fellowship of believers. (*silence*)

God, we have not taken care of the earth. We have not seen the needs of those around us and have failed to find you in the eyes of those who need us. (*silence*)

God, we have not given what we could have of our time, our money, our talents, and our gifts. Even while we acknowledge that all of these are from you, we have been afraid to give up what is not even ours. (*silence*)

God, like Peter, we have turned away from you and have denied that we are yours. Help us turn around, like Peter, and proclaimed you boldly to our friends and families. (*silence*)

God, we hesitate to follow you, for we do not know the way. (*silence*)

God, we ask for your forgiveness and seek your Holy Spirit to change our hearts and make us new. Amen.

Worship Service Reproducible Page